I0621842

Law Moms
Juggling Motherhood, Ambition & Personal Fulfillment

Sulit Press

Praise for *Law Moms: Juggling Motherhood, Ambition & Personal Fulfillment*

"This book is full of incredible stories written by strong, talented women. More than a brisk satisfying read about the challenges of being a woman, a lawyer, a mother and all the other hats we as women wear, it reminded me that there is really no limit to what women can do." —Barbara Toynes

"*Law Moms* is more than just a collection of narratives; it is a testament to the resilience, fortitude, and unwavering spirit of mothers in the legal profession. It is a beacon of hope for those grappling with similar struggles, offering reassurance, encouragement, and a reminder that together, we cannot only get through hard times but thrive.

Through these heartfelt accounts, readers are invited into the inner sanctum of the legal profession, where the demands of the courtroom collide with the joys and complexities of motherhood. These women bravely lay bare the multifaceted reality of their lives with unwavering honesty.

What sets this anthology apart is its ability to foster a profound sense of solidarity among its readers. As I delved into each story, I found echoes of my own experiences as a woman juggling my own solo law practice with motherhood and maintaining a sense of self. The shared struggles and joys depicted on these pages created a sense of camaraderie, reminding me that I am not alone in my journey." —Katherine A.E. Roe, Esq.

"Being a mom is hard work. Being a professional woman with children comes with an increased degree of difficulty. You want to win your case, protect your client and be that perfect spouse and attorney, but where does one place yourself and your sanity in this equation?

As a young mom and doctor, I always felt as though I was doing both jobs poorly. I am now near retirement, and have learned to give myself the love and compassion that I have given to others over the years.

I was impressed with what each author has so poignantly shared in their essays. You are all survivors of difficult situations and I am grateful to read of your life stories. Thank you for the courage to share your stories." —Linda Benjamin Soucie, MD

"As I delved into *Law Moms*, I found myself immediately captivated by the intricate balance these women navigate between their professional careers and the demands of motherhood. From the very first page, I was intrigued by the raw and honest accounts shared within its pages, unable to tear myself away from the engrossing narratives.I couldn't recommend *Law Moms* more highly. It's a compelling and thought-provoking read that offers a rare glimpse into the lives of working lawyer moms, leaving readers both inspired and enlightened. Whether you're a parent, a professional, or simply someone seeking a captivating story, this book is sure to leave a lasting impression." —Lori M Kerr

"*Law Moms* illuminates the unique life paths women take in becoming lawyers and mothers, and how those perspectives can shape legal careers. In these engaging stories, the authors share their personal and professional experiences, and in the process reveal some difficult truths and powerful insights that are universally valuable."
—Kim Van Winkle

"*Law Moms* provides refreshingly honest, beautiful, and inspiring stories from incredible women. I adored this collection of stories and the important topics discussed throughout the book. There's a variety of stories and perspectives on motherhood, their passion for law, and their experiences with balancing both. Although I'm not a mom, I could relate to some of the stories and their honesty made me feel less alone in my experiences." —Teresa Cortes

"Excellent book that shares the raw and honest struggles we face as women lawyers, especially as mom lawyers. While reading many of the stories, I thought "this sounds like my story." So refreshing to know that we are not alone on this incredibly rewarding yet challenging journey."
—Mary-Ellen King

"In my life, I keep finding that mothering is a world class sport. When I meet a mom who is also a lawyer, I am always floored because these women are badasses. This book explores motherhood through the lens of a historically misogynistic and demanding role. The women in this book have each opened their hearts to share vulnerable tales of where they could literally be doing everything right and yet still feel the pressure of the world to be more and have it all together. I hope you take time, no matter if you're a lawyer or not (I am sure not as smart as these women!) to read this and get a better understanding of working motherhood or simply see yourself in their stories. Buckle up for honesty, transparency, and a bunch of 'yes, girl.'" —Claire Frisby

Paperback: 979-8-9880332-8-8

Ebook: 979-8-9880332-7-1

Edited by Erin Althaus, Kristi Koeter, and Michelle Savage

Cover art by Christy Jaynes

Sulit Press

www.sulitpress.com

Ready to fast-track your publishing career, increase your visibility, or boost your business?

Harness the power of partnership by contributing a 3,000-word chapter to one of our upcoming Multi-Author Books!

If you are...

Inspired by what you do and want to generously share what you've learned...

Committed to meeting deadlines and doing your best work...

Ready to connect with other aspiring authors who are as excited as you are to share your book with the world...

Then our Multi-Author Book might be the right path for you!

Learn more at https://www.sulitpress.com/

Contents

Introduction

In the heart of every woman who pursues a career in law lies a compelling narrative, a unique blend of motivation, aspiration, and guts. The decision to navigate the rigorous path of the legal profession *and* the profound journey of motherhood requires a motherlode of strength and dedication, and a relentless pursuit of balance. This collection of stories is an exploration of the downright demanding legal profession and the equally challenging yet rewarding realm of motherhood.

Women are drawn to the legal profession for countless reasons, each as diverse as the women themselves. For many, the allure lies in the pursuit of justice, advocating for those without a voice and striving toward social change. Others are captivated by the intellectual rigor and the dynamic challenges that the law presents, offering a career that never ceases to evolve, challenge, and inspire. The legal field promises not just a platform for advocacy and intellectual fulfillment but also opens doors to further opportunities, financial stability, and the potential for influence and autonomy. Behind these motivations lies a deeper drive, a passion for the law, and its capacity to transform lives and societies.

Out of all the possible pathways one could take, there's no way of knowing if life as a lawyer will be worth the effort or even remotely resemble how it was originally imagined. The demands are enormous, and the women who pursue this path must navigate a complex legal landscape filled with obstacles and even heartbreak. They must contend with systemic biases, long hours, and the weight of responsibility inherent in advocating for others.

For those who embrace motherhood, the legal profession becomes a stage for an even more complex balancing act. The stories within this anthology reflect the multifaceted experiences of women who juggle court dates with school runs, client meetings with bedtime stories, and trial preparations with the endless quest for work-life harmony. These narratives shine a light on the resilience of women who pursue the high stakes of legal battles and the tender moments of family life with equal fervor.

In this collection, eight women candidly share what it means to take on two of the hardest jobs in the world—mom and lawyer. Among these stories, you'll encounter:

- A second-generation lawyer confronting her relationship with alcohol and its pervasive influence in legal culture.

- A mother of three who embraces imperfection as she opts to join her youngest kids' summer musical.

- A woman who takes refuge in a law career as she tirelessly advocates for an adopted son with severe behavioral issues while trying to protect her younger daughter.

- A trailblazer challenging cultural stigmas surrounding mental health and therapy while battling depression.

- A personal injury lawyer finding solace amid her demanding schedule, cherishing precious moments with her children while helping her clients seek justice.

Law Moms is not just an exploration of the challenges and triumphs faced by women at the intersection of motherhood and law; it is a celebration of their strength, their victories, and their unwavering commitment to both their families and their careers. Through these stories, you'll find inspiration and perhaps a newfound appreciation of these remarkable women who demonstrate passion and perseverance.

Welcome to a journey through the lives of women who exemplify what it means to balance the scales.

1
Bit by Bit

Susan Arenella

They were pale blue booklets, as I recall, filled with frantic hand scrawl, my nerve-shot responses to the lofty legal questions posed by our professors. The last page of each booklet featured the final grade—the bad news, I came to call it—scribbled in red, circled several times for emphasis. As if first year law school wasn't brutal enough, these exams were worse. During the long semester preceding them, we were given no quizzes. We received no guidance to help gauge whether we understood the ambiguities of tort law or what the Rule Against Perpetuities really meant. For each subject, there was only one test at semester's end. One shot. No makeups, no extra credit, no chatting up the professor, angling for a second chance.

And yet, in the swirling brew of first year chaos, our teachers believed the cream would rise, that the brightest legal stars would simply emerge from the pages of those pale blue booklets. Our first semester exam grades were to be calculated into a grade point average, then cruelly displayed at the tops of our resumes, right under our names. God forbid we should waste the time of some busy law partner, flown in by his firm to interview a law clerk worth hiring. Only those with stellar first-year grades would qualify. They'd be wined and dined and golfed with, and ultimately receive post-graduation job offers from some of the most prestigious law firms in the nation. To be clear, I didn't want one of those soul-sucking jobs. What I did want at the end of my first year of law school—no, what I expected—was the opportunity to turn a few of those fancy law firms down.

The previous June, I had graduated from an honors program at a top California university, an achievement eked out while raising three girls and helping run the janitorial company my husband and I had built from scratch. I was told I had a knack for writing, which garnered me high grades through undergrad and praise from my professors, culminating with the coveted Outstanding Thesis Award. So, I arrived at law school a bit haughty, anticipating what I thought would be a three-year engagement as the Woman Who Had Her Shit Together. But as my pale blue booklets piled up that spring, they confirmed what my roiling gut and rosacea outbreaks had been telling me all year: I was a mediocre law student at best. That burbling sound?

It was me, flailing beneath the cream, sinking to the bottom of the bowl.

"So, your husband tells me you're in law school," Dede said.

I forced a tight smile at my girls' theater teacher, her eyes aglint with awe. Clearly, she hadn't seen my grades. I glanced around the sweaty studio, searching amid a gaggle of bouncing adolescents for my youngest two. *Damn that Joe,* I thought. *He tells everyone.* But I couldn't complain. He had been a prince that year, shuffling the girls off to school and soccer games and theater practice while I hunched over obscenely thick law books, studying for the As I didn't get.

"You'd be perfect for the summer musical," Dede continued. "We're doing *The Velveteen Rabbit*. We need someone to play the boy's mother."

I flashed her a *why me* squint. Dede was a petite woman, but also a force, with short-cropped hair and a wide smile. She slid around the room—shoulders back, chin up—like a former dancer might, possessing a remarkable ability to tune out the cacophony around her. But I hardly knew this woman. Until recently, Joe had been picking up our girls, both of whom had now run to my side and were listening in.

"The mother is a busy lawyer," Dede went on, "who doesn't have time for her children."

I could have sunk into the dusty floorboards. I deserved that. I had all but abandoned the girls that year, attending required classes from eight to five each day. At first, I tried to study at home, after dinner while the dog barked and dirty pans clanked in the sink and the girls tromped up and down the stairs, asking homework questions. I eventually started holing up in the law library after class, at Joe's insistence, reading for the next day's humiliations until ten or eleven or twelve. Sleep became a distant memory.

"Ooh," Sarah said, grabbing my arm. "Say yes." At fourteen, I was surprised she didn't hate me by now, she *and* Lizy. It had been a difficult year for all of us. New neighborhood, new schools, new friends. Nine months of tacos or their father's valiant attempts at dinner. At one point, Joe decided we should be vegetarians, which for him meant whipping up large batches of Mediterranean tabouli every week, a staple he packed into the girls' lunches daily until they cornered me, wide-eyed and desperate. "Please make it stop," they begged. "No more tabouli."

Yet apparently, the girls still missed me. And I missed them. I missed our life.

"Well," I chuckled at Dede. "I *was* voted most likely to succeed on Broadway in the eighth grade."

I could feel my cheeks flush. *Where did that come from?* Yes, I had grown up loving Julie Andrews and every musical known to man. I had even created a few as a child, borrowing songs from Mary Poppins and other musicals, putting on shows in the backyard, under the swing-set-turned-stage. But I hardly ever talked about those dream-swelled *before* days, especially with people I didn't know.

Dede blinked, unimpressed with my junior high credentials.

"Do it, do it, do it," my girls chanted, like frat boys at a beer bash.

Of course, taking the role would mean being available, not just for rehearsals, but for the musical itself, which would run in a local theater for a few days and nights in August. I'd have no time for the all-important summer legal job I had yet to secure, the job that the woman in the career office framed as my last hope for a passable legal resume, a partial deliverance from the mediocre grades in my pale blue booklets. Cue that distant burbling sound.

"Sure," I shrugged at Dede, and squeals erupted. Ponytails bobbed.

I had a vague recollection of *The Velveteen Rabbit* from reading it to the girls when they were little: the boy and his stuffed toy rabbit who longed to be real, who, in the end, became real. There was a fairy involved at some point, plus the boy's unconditional love for the rabbit, a combination that, as fairy tales go, eventually changed everything. But I couldn't remember a mother in the story, busy lawyer or otherwise. And if we ever owned the book, we didn't now. So, with my brain still buzzing in study mode, I stopped at the local library on the way home. I told the girls we needed a solid understanding of the material prior to our first practice. They rolled their eyes.

Sarah and Lizy loved musicals. They'd been chirping out Disney songs since they were toddlers, as did many kids, I suppose. But they also sang the old show tunes, from Broadway as well as movies. They actually knew who Gene Kelly was, and Danny Kaye. So, enrolling them in this theater group had probably been the best move we'd made in months, the perfect antidote to a year of upheaval.

We had moved from Southern California to Austin the previous July, caravanning across the blazing desert, Joe in the giant moving truck, me in the Volvo. Sarah was thirteen at the time, and Lizy, ten. Jessica, our twenty-year-old, tagged along too, but she hightailed it back to California after sweating through her first triple-digit summer.

"You people are crazy," she said.

And maybe we were. Some might have called it ill-advised for us to sell our home and our thriving business, to pull our children away from their friends and out of the school they loved, just so I could go to law school. But Joe and I were the masters of ill-advised decisions.

We had exchanged vows fourteen years previous on a humid July morning in a friend's backyard, two months after Joe's eighteenth birthday, and only three days after he finished Marine Corps boot camp. I was twenty-one. As we stood before a small gathering of skeptical onlookers, promising 'til death do us part, we tallied up, between the two of us, one six-year-old-daughter (mine), one high school diploma (his), no money, no car, and no reasonable explanation for the rush. I wasn't even pregnant. Regardless, when Joe got stationed at Camp Pendleton three months later, I quit my job as a hairstylist and left the shuttered East Coast mill town where I'd lived all my life, following him to California with Jessica in tow.

"How Hard Can It Be?" we laughed in those early days, like a mantra, our faces tilted toward that warm winter sun. I cringe at that mantra now, so reckless, so defiant, like we were hurling a gauntlet at fate. We lived off base then, in Oceanside. All Joe's meager pay could afford was a roach-infested apartment in a rundown area called The Strand, where surfers piled mattresses into sandy shacks and junkies roamed the streets, shooting up in the laundry room, leaving their needles behind. But we dug in. After all, California had palm trees.

Things didn't start turning around until after the Marines, when we moved to Orange County, where Joe and I launched wholehearted efforts to better ourselves and put each other through college. We lived in "married student housing" then, the college's euphemism for a dingy trailer park on the side of the 55 Freeway. There, we built our cleaning business, which enabled us to buy the Volvo and a modest ranch house in Santa Ana. All told, it took us fourteen years to build a good life in California. A stable life of moderate means. And I had just uprooted it, willy nilly, to go to law school, when there were perfectly good schools on the West Coast offering me a spot.

Which was how I found myself marching into an Austin acting studio that June having "done the reading," as they say in law school, fully familiarized with *The Velveteen Rabbit*. There were layers to the fairy tale I'd never noticed while reading it to my sleepy young girls at bedtime, when I'd be nodding off myself. Yes, the boy's love helps the toy rabbit become real, but the story conveys a deeper struggle for authenticity and self-acceptance. On the rabbit's long journey, he questions real and strives for real, eventually convincing himself he *is* real. But he loses almost everything in the process: his fur, his velvet nose, even the little boy who loved him. In fact, by the time the fairy arrives, Velveteen is spent. He has nothing to offer her but a desire to be real, and his flawed, whiskerless self. Still, she waves her wand.

In the stage version, I would be playing an overworked criminal defense attorney with three kids and a corporate-type husband who was absent through most of the musical on some never-ending business trip. But I wasn't the only adult in the play. There was an aunt, an uncle, and a grandfather, the latter played by alternating actors: an older man with kind eyes who worked in a hospice, and a calm, middle-aged hippy type on break from the School of Social Work. A woman lawyer, recently retired, played the boy's grandmother. We all had a child or two in the musical, which lent our presence a certain plausibility. But still, I felt silly. Sure, it was summer, but weren't there more important things for us grown-ups to be doing?

Some things differed between the musical and the book, but much was the same: a stuffed rabbit, gifted to the boy at Christmas, shoved into a nursery with fancier toys— dolls with bending limbs, motorized cars, and tanks with moving hulls—who snubbed Velveteen for being so plain, for not being as functional or as real as they were. The script changed the wise, old skin horse of the book to a modernized Rex the Lion, who embraced Velveteen, who explained how nursery magic worked: that if a child really, really loved a toy, the toy would become real.

"Does it happen all at once," the little girl playing Velveteen would query, her blue eyes sparkling under the studio's buzzing fluorescent lights. "Or bit by bit?"

"It doesn't happen all at once," the young boy playing Rex would answer in a low, sage-sounding voice. "You become. It takes a long time."

This was a vital scene, rehearsed ad nauseum, while we adults traded winks and patronizing smiles as if to say: *Aren't they cute?* Because we were grown-ups after all, with demanding jobs and impossible bosses, with real spouses and houses full of kids, with real mortgages and doctor bills and worries and regrets. We were up to our eyeballs in real.

As summer unfolded, so did the heat, blanketing Austin with triple digits I still couldn't get used to. The practice studio was old, the air conditioning patchy, unable to cool a confined space filled with so much singing and dancing and tumbling around. We adults would sit on the sidelines, sweat beading on our foreheads, watching the kids practice, waiting for our parts.

Sarah played the oldest child, a pouty teenager who hated babysitting her siblings and complained I was never home. Lizy appeared in different scenes. She was a cousin at the Christmas Celebration, and a kid at the Summer Picnic in the Park. She also played one of the real bunnies (rapping gangsta bunnies, in this iteration) who stumbled upon Velveteen in the park, taunting him for his inability to hop, his lack of real fur. This was the *aha* moment in play, in which a despondent Velveteen realizes the boy's love could only take him so far.

I had two scenes with the girls: the Christmas Celebration and the Summer Picnic in the Park. I also had a solo part, talking on the phone to my far-flung husband (whose trip had been extended yet again), and another near-solo, hovering over my sick son as he lay unconscious in his bed. So, was I any good in this musical? Not really. I was stiff and inhibited, self-conscious in my flowy dresses and too-big shorts, purchased because I'd outgrown all my California clothes, having gained twenty pounds in law school. Dede never criticized (because it's hard to find adults who'll sign up to humiliate themselves in public). But my less-than-stellar performance made me wonder: Maybe my old junior high classmates had gotten it wrong. Maybe I never would've made it on Broadway, or off Broadway, or anywhere, even if my innocent *before* days hadn't ended so abruptly.

I'd had a happyish childhood of the Irish Catholic variety: a June Cleaver mother, a cop for a father, a priest for an uncle, and a stern, rosary-toting grandmother with a large extended family. These were the aunts, uncles, and cousins I grew up around—a sturdy lot of firemen, nurses, and teachers—who were always running in and out, forever sipping tea around our kitchen table. And I was the literal drama queen of the family, with my continuous singing and dancing, my made-up musicals.

My father was my biggest fan, always urging me to practice again and again, convincing me I could make a career out of it. But then he died, suddenly, violently, when I was twelve. The dancing and singing stopped. And over time I devolved, from the Girl Most Likely to Succeed on Broadway into the role I would assume for the next few years: Angry Young Girl Looking for Parties (and also, a father). I'd roam the streets costumed to the hilt, in black satin pants and glittered platforms, just like David Bowie's. There were drugs involved, all kinds, and guys too, older ones, including the married twenty-five-year-old with whom I planned to abscond until I got pregnant and he left without me. I was fifteen.

"You know what this makes you, right?"

Did my uncle the priest actually say this to me when my pregnancy came to light, after the vanished guy's wife told my family? These were turbulent times; I might've heard him wrong. But I snapped back nonetheless, something about Jesus loving Mary Magdalene anyway. Whatever he said, and whatever he meant, this marked the start of the judgment, the beginning of the shame.

Soon after, my mortified mother shuttled me off to a Catholic maternity home, certain the nuns would convince me to give the baby up. But they didn't. So, she reluctantly offered to take me and the baby in, provided I quit high school, get a trade, and move out. A kind offer, which came at a price: other than my grandmother and my uncle the priest, the rest of our extended Irish brood—the aunts and uncles and cousins who'd been circling me all my life, like so many bees around a hive—disappeared. Because it was one thing to be "in trouble," as my grandmother called it, but quite another to bring that trouble home for all the world to see.

I graduated from cosmetology school a scant year later, got a job as a stylist, and moved into a third-floor attic space in a crooked tenement near the railroad bridge. Then, I applied for food stamps, which heaped shame upon shame. I could hear the palpable hush whenever I pulled them out in the grocery store, especially from the shoppers behind, whose eyes would dart between me and the squealing conveyor belt, quietly judging my potatoes and carrots, my macaroni and cheese.

"Fuck 'em," I'd whisper as I walked back to my tenement, in that brash East Coast way I spoke back then. I thought I was tough in those days, invincible. And I believed it was that easy, to repel the shame, to let the disgust and rejection bounce off me like sparks from a flame. But I didn't repel the shame. I swallowed it. And I carried it with me to California, none the wiser, much like the grief I had no words for.

It took a while in California to become the Woman Who Had Her Shit Together. I didn't realize the role was available to me until I started going to community college in Orange County—a class here, a class there, an education cobbled together, bit by bit. But my observations outside the classroom proved just as crucial. I started noticing those California women with their manicured nails and suntanned arms, with their perfect blonde haircuts and sleek Volvo station wagons, from which tumbled their towheaded children in pricey surfer garb and brand-name sneakers. Did I want to be like them? Not at all. But they lived in a different world, a world I'd never had entrance to.

"I'll show them," I thought, not the California women, but those forgotten people back home, who had rejected me and judged me, who now surfaced like phantoms from some cobwebbed corner in my mind. Shame burrows deep. And so, we grew the business. We bought the Volvo. We moved out of the trailer park and into the house and enrolled the girls in dance class and piano lessons. I worked hard and studied harder, accumulating As, applying to law school. Noble pursuits all. But somewhere along the way, my reasoning had shifted. I was no longer bettering myself; I was proving myself to an unseen group of people long in the past. Perfectly, I might add. Because shame, my brand, anyway, demanded perfection. In the process, I moved further and further away from that girl in the crooked tenement and her glaring imperfections, eventually rejecting her entirely, just as she had been rejected. What could she possibly offer a Woman Who Had Her Shit Together?

Law school was rife with perfectionists. I assumed I'd fit right in. However, the career office labeled me a *returning student*, which sounds benign, but when you are stumbling through the hallways with a herd of fresh-faced twenty-somethings, the term feels vaguely pejorative, like secret code for *old lady on campus*. Some of my younger cohorts confirmed this sentiment. There was the dark-haired sorority-type girl, who kept calling me Mrs. Arenella, who asked me, "What do you do for fun, PTA?" Then there was the blue-eyed MIT grad who kept telling me I looked tired, who said I'd have to learn to "run with the young pups" if I planned to survive. I shrugged it off at first. But the snarky comments, the long days of study, and those pale blue booklets eventually reduced me to a depleted, weeping lump of a woman who wanted nothing more than to wake up and be back in California. Magical thinking, I suppose. But I was desperate.

To me, I was failing at everything: being a mother, being a wife, being a student, being myself.

And so, the musical. I don't recall how many practices we had each week. I only remember the all-consuming blur of a Volvo full of kids, mine and the ones I offered to pick up, singing Broadway tunes at decibel ten as I drove to and from the studio in the unrelenting heat. But I didn't mind. Who gets to do this? Plunge into their daughters' world at an age when they're usually pushing you away?

It was a wild summer, a mad jumble of flubbed lines and missed cues, of adults fumbling through their roles, of kids singing and leaping and cartwheeling across the studio. A few months earlier, I would've run from such chaos, blessing Dede for being such a saint. But now, I just stood on the sidelines, stilled by the spectacle, watching the kids, thinking: *Was I ever like this, in the before days? So uninhibited? So oblivious to the eyes of others?* Maybe the heat had dulled my senses, or perhaps it was the repetition of it all, rehearsing the same lines again and again. Either way, I grew to love every minute of that crazy production, where nothing was perfect, but everything seemed right.

It was temporary, of course. Soon, I would return to law school, to the students and the study and the strain. And a musical fairy tale, on its own, wouldn't have the power to cure me of my perfectionism once and for all. But it would provide some perspective. Over the next two years, I'd spend less time at the library and more weekends with Joe and the girls. On better days, I would try to be more realistic, a little less obsessed with reaching for a perfection I could never attain. I'd perch at a desk in the half moon seating of our classroom, watching those top-graded students across from me, with their fierce eyes and oh-so-observant answers. And I'd wonder who their phantoms were. Who or what was driving them to some unreachable perfection?

Eventually, I would graduate and get a job, despite my mediocre grades, my lack of a summer clerkship. In fact, the musical would be my selling point, the much-needed punchline in stodgy law firm interviews. "I didn't work in a law office that summer," I'd shrug. "But I played a lawyer on stage."

On opening night, we arrived early at the theater-in-the-round, already costumed for the first scene: the Christmas Celebration. It was a dark, circular stage, surrounded by bleacher seating. Three small balcony stages hovered above the circle, set between the seats occupied by parents and friends, and friends of friends. It was a full house. When the lights came up on the Christmas scene, Sarah stomped out first, the teenage sister in a velvet dress, grousing at her younger brother and sister to clean up. I entered the stage soon after, rushed and annoyed, collecting toys and discarded gift wrap as the happy guests filed in. Lizy was among them. It was a lively holiday scene, with gifts and hugs and laughter, which, being a musical, eventually erupted into song. Right before the song, I climbed the stairs of the balcony.

This was where the Christmas tree stood, which I was supposed to decorate as I sang with the others. I turned and faced the actors below as I fussed with a branch on the tree. There, I spotted them—Sarah, Lizy—red-lipped and rosy-cheeked in their stage makeup, singing out toward the packed house. *My girls,* I thought. It was a proud moment, a mother moment. But then came the next thought, which surfaced unbidden: *They look like bookends on that stage, on either side of the age I was when everything fell apart.*

Perhaps adrenaline unearthed this thought, all those lights and faces, my jangling nerves. Regardless, I'd never realized this before. In fact, until then, I'd never given any conscious thought to my past. My gaze followed Sarah in her velvet dress as she ascended the stairs to join me. *Fourteen,* I thought. *Young for her age, a bit of a late bloomer. But still. Was I ever fourteen? The last thing I remembered was being twelve. And then I wasn't.*

I'm not a believer in made-for-TV moments where everything turns around in one fell swoop. Life is too messy for tidy epiphanies. And there certainly weren't any that night. No magic fairy, waving her wand. It would take a long time for me to tackle my perfectionism and even longer to confront the deep-seated shame propelling it—years, really—plus enough counseling to arguably buy my future therapist a boat. But in time, I would unravel the Woman Who Had Her Shit Together, just as I had created her, bit by bit. I would learn to gather up the disparate parts of who I was and who I had become, to embrace and accept and hold space for each of them: the woman, the wife, the mother, the lawyer, and that brave teenage girl in the crooked tenement who thought she was invincible.

But for a moment on that stage, I *did* feel something: a glimpse, a glimmer, the first realization that I had been carrying way too much for way too long. And then it was gone. Sarah ascended the balcony just as the song was ending. I winked at my daughter on the other side of the Christmas tree, then eyed Lizy below, swaying and singing in her green floral dress. Together, we reached out toward the audience to bring home that final note, right on cue, while the youngest actors twirled around us, as kids tend to do, weightless almost, and so impossibly carefree.

Susan Arenella

S usan Arenella is a wife, a mother, a lawyer, and a writer. She has practiced law for twenty-five years, mostly as a government attorney battling Medicaid fraud. Her last position was as Director of Investigation for the Civil Medicaid Fraud Division of the Texas Attorney General's Office. There, she led multi-state teams of lawyers in the investigation of whistleblower lawsuits filed against Big Pharma and other national healthcare providers, which resulted in several multimillion-dollar recoveries for Texas and other states.

She now writes full-time and is working on a forthcoming memoir about motherhood, the complexities of adoption, and her prior escapades in Lawrence, Massachusetts, the East Coast mill town where she grew up. Susan currently lives in Austin, Texas, with her husband, Joe, and Sylvester, a neighborhood cat whom she houses and feeds but swears is not hers.

https://www.linkedin.com/in/susanarenella/

https://www.facebook.com/susanarenella.writer/

https://www.instagram.com/susanarenella/

2
Asylum

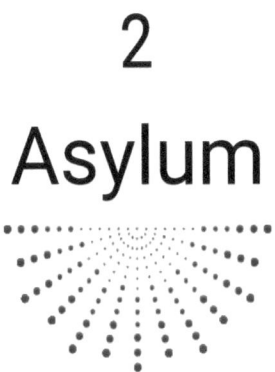

Abigail Seymour

The back of my baby's head thuds against my chest with surprising force. I cry out, worried that something has startled him or he has hurt himself, and I can't see his face. He is buckled into a blue baby carrier, facing away from me, arms and legs dangling like a skydiver from a parachute.

I have been walking slowly to and fro in the airport gate area, bouncing gently and patting his belly through the fabric. Now, I walk over to a reflective store window so I can see him. He blinks back at me, with his perfect tear-free brown eyes—and then lifts his chin without breaking eye contact and thumps me again with the back of his head. He pauses, still looking at me, then starts kicking the tops of my legs and hitting my chest at the same time, like someone kicking a horse to make it move. When I start pacing again, he stops.

We are in Guatemala City, waiting for a flight back to the United States. I met my son a few hours earlier for the first time when the adoption coordinator handed him to me along with a small jar of pureed baby food and a spit-up cloth. She kissed the top of his head, mumbled a few words into his hair, and then left him with me. Forever.

How could I have possibly known, in those early days and months, that this perfect, precious nine-month-old baby would continue to kick and hit and defy me and everyone around him every day for the next decade and beyond? Even in the airport, when Diego (not his real name) was still small enough for me to tote around on my chest, he was controlling where we would both go.

I was not at all accustomed to recalibrating my life's route to one set by anyone else. At nearly forty years old, I knew that having children "changes your life," but I thought that meant that they join the life that you are already living. They come along on hikes and beach trips, giggle as you hoist them on your shoulders, and share in licking chocolate frosting off the spoon while you gaze adoringly at each other. You work, they play, you play together, then you whisper Big Truths to them about life and being a good person, and they make construction paper hearts for you to put on your fridge.

I was not prepared to have a child who would tell me he was going to ask Santa for a gun so he could kill me. I was not prepared to get pregnant during the adoption process and have two very small kids who were only fifteen months apart in age. I was not prepared to spend the next ten years keeping one child safe from the other, researching everything I could find about Oppositional Defiant Disorder and Reactive Attachment Disorder. I was not prepared to have to work especially hard on bad days to resist driving off alone in my white Kia minivan and swerving into oncoming traffic.

When we adopted Diego, my husband and I had been married for seven years and, despite "trying," were not able to conceive. Adoption was an easy decision for us both. Neither one of us knew the first thing about taking care of kids; however, since I was the youngest of five and a wanderer, and he had spent most of his life collecting advanced degrees and hiking mountain trails by himself, we figured we would just learn as we go and hope for the best.

I was ready to settle down—I had been to college, lived and worked in New York City, traveled abroad, and built a modest career in photography and freelance writing. I had briefly considered law school years before, but I was such a free spirit that it seemed too straight a path for me. Besides, I wasn't smart enough. "You could probably *marry* a lawyer," my mom had said once, "but I don't think you could *be* a lawyer." I believed her, sadly, but also vowed that if I ever became a mother, I would never say such limiting things to my children.

Diego was the only person who had no faith in himself or what he could do. Whether this was a genetic disposition or the result of being removed from his country and his biological family is a mystery that remains unsolved. He was one of more than 30,000 children adopted from Guatemala between the mid-1990s and 2008. For all of our due diligence in making the decision to adopt from Guatemala, neither my husband nor I had any inkling that we were participating in a program rotten to the core with corruption, graft, and allegations of human trafficking. Adoptions were shut down just after Diego came home when Guatemala became a signatory to the Hague Inter-country Adoption Convention. At the time, though, we knew only that we loved our sweet boy, that he had been born healthy, and his unmarried birth mother had willingly relinquished him in adoption. There was no information as to why, and in the paperwork, she emphatically asked not to be contacted. Her only message to her child's future adoptive parents was: "Please send my baby to school."

That brief trip to Guatemala and the knowledge later of how few options existed for indigenous women was the beginning of unearthing my buried dream of becoming a lawyer. Overcoming my imposter syndrome and belief that I wasn't smart enough took a few years more. I was certainly angry enough to become a lawyer by then, seeing how the law was abused and ignored to finagle shady adoptions abroad, how the women who came from the Guatemalan Highlands could either give up their children in adoption or risk being raped and robbed on a treacherous journey to seek asylum in the US.

My sense of duty to protect this baby, whose mother had taken such grave risks to make sure he got to us, was profound. And when I gave birth to a little girl, my sense of duty to protect her was equally fierce. For a short time, I could carry both kids in my arms, one on each hip, and would dance around the kitchen with them, laughing.

But everything shifted when Diego was around five years old and began exhibiting troubling behaviors. He would get angry and say not just "I hate you," but "I want to die you." He would get quiet and hoard odd things, including once, his sister's Epipen, which we only found when he screamed in pain from having accidentally pierced his thumb with its needle. He couldn't be comforted; he would arch his back to snuggles, turn away from eye contact, and in toy sections, he was drawn to images and games with dark, sinister themes. He was expelled from preschool for biting and for refusing to comply with the teachers' gentle requests to sit on the carpet for storytime. His little sister, Willa (also not her real name), stopped speaking around that same time and was later diagnosed with selective mutism, a form of extreme anxiety caused often by a traumatic incident. She went almost two years without speaking to anyone outside our immediate family.

I don't remember the first time Diego became dysregulated while out in public, but I do remember when we stopped going places in order to try and minimize it happening. An explosive rage episode is much more than a tantrum; it is a whirling dervish of curse words, objects hurled, and, if it happens in public, deer-in-headlights parents. People are quick to say that a child like Diego just needs a swift smack to the backside to get him in line. "What that boy needs is a 'whoopin'," I would overhear. But those same people will be the first to report a parent to child protective services. One especially loud episode in a store prompted a bystander to do just that. Two nice officers came to our house a few hours later to do a welfare check on Diego. After showing them that he was fine, I wanted to tell them that he had recently punched me in the eye and bitten my arm. I covered the round bite mark with my sleeve while also wondering if I could ask them to come check on the rest of us every now and then.

Between his dark episodes, though, Diego was curious, loving, and sweet—he liked catching minnows in the local creek or listening to me read a book to him and his sister. He especially loved *Runaway Bunny,* about the mom who goes off in search of her wayward child.

"'If you run away,' said his mother, 'I will run after you. For you are my little bunny.'"

"Read it again," Diego would say, looking up at me from where he was leaning against my arm. In those little moments, I would have a glimmer of hope that connections were being made and synapses healed, and we were out of the woods. Alas, within an hour or so, Diego's expression would change and his pupils would seem to flatten, the same steady gaze I remembered from the airport all those years ago. He would throw things: shoes, books, glass picture frames, dishes. Willa would run and hide in her room as we tried our best to find out what had upset him. Sometimes, it was being told that it was time to turn off the TV or that we would get ice cream tomorrow after school, but not right this minute.

Each milestone in Diego's life gave him a little more freedom and control, however, which seemed to buoy him for a brief time. He was happy when he realized he could walk on his own, ride a bike, or finally be old enough to ride in the front seat of the car. But being corrected, denied, and limited in some way was to trigger a defense mechanism that came from somewhere way down deep.

Whether I was the proxy for the birth mother whom he had lost or a stand-in for the world that blocked his way, Diego seemed to reserve most of his vitriol just for me. The walls of our house were pocked with holes from all those objects hurled over the years; there was still a piece of splintered wood from where he used the back of a hammer to pierce his sister's locked bedroom door.

To make matters worse, my husband and I couldn't agree on how to help Diego once it became clear that he was deeply unhappy, existentially drowning, and we were all going down with him. Whatever unknown pre-birth or pre-memory trauma he may have endured had now been passed along to all of us. My husband and I would have tense, late-night whispered disagreements about how to proceed, what to do the next time Diego started to explode. Even if we agreed in the moment, I would find myself standing alone during the next meltdown while my husband would do and give anything, *anything,* to make it stop. If my "no" was setting it off, then my husband would rush in with "yes"—yes to the gummy bears, the new toy, the video game, the donuts.

We learned to run two separate families under one roof, switching off one-on-one time with each child as best we could. As Diego entered his pre-teen years, knives and scissors were kept out of reach, and parental controls were installed on electronic devices. He somehow already knew about the dark web and vaping and porn. He racked up $1,000 on my credit card once using Fortnite coins before I discovered it and blocked the game, which caused another explosion. We were losing ground, and I was losing my mind.

After we had already made the rounds of kind child therapists with their squishy balls and fidget toys, none of whom were much help, I tried occupational therapy, non-stimulant ADHD medications, and stimulant medications; I eliminated all processed foods for everyone, making homemade loaves of flavorless bread to cut out white flour, sugar, dyes. But Diego would always manage to get his hands on some candy or other that was made entirely of red dye #9 and sugar.

I tried a "screen fast," removing all TVs, phones, and tablets from our lives. I tried dry brushing techniques and weighted blankets. When it became clear he was so oppositional that he wouldn't actually go to a therapy appointment, one kind counselor offered to come to the house instead. Diego gave him the dead-eye stare. My husband would sigh heavily and say simply, "Nobody can help us."

In a last-ditch attempt to finally get to the bottom of what was going on, I checked Diego into the child psychiatric unit at a prestigious teaching hospital when he was eleven. A team of doctors and residents observed Diego for a month, and finally put him on an antidepressant and discharged him with no diagnosis other than "he doesn't display much empathy." I am not unconvinced that his disquietude was made worse by the windowless lockdown unit, the days with nothing to do, and people asking probing questions. Boy, Interrupted. I was out of ideas.

Somewhere between the dry brushing and the child psychiatric unit is when I reset my own coordinates and headed toward becoming a lawyer. It didn't feel healthy for me to be SO invested in my children, and clearly over-invested in Diego. The more

I focused on him and on trying to figure him out, the more miserable we all became. So I went to law school.

I wanted to prove to myself that the drive I had to help my children survive this life could propel me to a life of my own with a larger purpose. The darkness that threatened to overcome our family made me so angry that I grabbed onto something outside the house, outside myself, outside of our family to escape it. I became driven to help women find their way to freedom, whether it was from their country or from an abusive home life or from an unhappy marriage. If I was going to become someone who could help, I had to design my own escape route first.

I found asylum in the law. I loved the heavy books, the cases I had to read, the professors (many of whom were younger than I was), and the long lectures and readings. I loved going for an hour or more without thinking about what might happen to my children when they were older, what might happen to them tomorrow. But mostly, I loved that nobody knew me at all. I could start my story all over again.

My first year of law school, the kids were in second and third grades, respectively. I took their first day of school pictures and then jumped in front of the camera myself, grinning and holding a sign that said, "First day of 17th grade."

I would toggle back and forth daily between focusing on my studies and being a mom, sometimes only partially succeeding at each. I interned at the law school's humanitarian immigration law clinic, where I learned about the IR-3 visa that had brought Diego to the US, read about the Hague Convention treaty that stopped Guatemalan adoptions, and the asylum laws that women from Guatemala were invoking at the border. I read about juvenile justice, mental health law, and child protective services cases.

I remember pacing outside the law school during Torts class so I could talk to the admissions director of an alternative school. I was describing how "non-traditional" a learner Diego was, how brilliant and creative, that he could play a Mozart piano piece by ear, and had once built a two-foot long pirate ship of his own design out of Legos. (I left out the part about him building a structurally correct pistol out of the same Legos a day later.) He was getting in trouble at his public school, and I was getting frequent calls from the principal.

I was hopeful, then, since we were going to match Diego's creative, restless spirit with a place that could actually accommodate him—this free-thinking school had mixed age groups in each classroom, lots of outdoor time, and, best of all, a mission to promote peace and justice through education.

At around eleven-thirty in the morning of his first day at the new school, the front office called me to come pick him up. "Is he OK?" I asked.

"Yes, he is OK," she answered, "but this just isn't a good fit." When I probed for more information, she told me that when asked to go sit at a desk, Diego had told the teacher to go fuck himself.

I stumbled through those three years, nearly dropping out more than once due to missing class to attend IEP meetings or to take Willa to her therapy since the stress at home was causing her to have panic attacks. It was becoming clear that my marriage couldn't hold up to the battering of our constantly clashing views on how to parent Diego. I couldn't just ignore it when he hid his sister's asthma inhaler, saying he would only give it back if I paid him. He was as tall as I was, and his anger was no longer directed only at inanimate objects. When I told him calmly that he was not allowed to call me a c#&*t, he lunged at me and shoved me against the wall, the back of my head snapping back with a thud.

It was very hard to face the fact that I repeatedly asked—*begged*—my husband to choose our family as a whole over just Diego, and he had declined. We were a triangle, not a circle, and Diego had a sharp corner all to himself. But he was not incapable of participating in life, as he had shown on occasion. He was a behavioral outlier, yes, but he was also sharp as a tack, not to mention strategic. My years of watching him calibrate his behavior for others and in settings that suited him (chess matches or at a part-time job bagging groceries, for example) confirmed for me that he was reserving certain kinds of behaviors—the cruelest ones—just for us. I took little comfort in knowing that this was because he felt safe with us (that's what a therapist told us).

My husband simply did not think that Diego was capable of civil interaction with the outside world. He felt it was best that he remained safely isolated at home, sitting at his command post where he played video games all day, bellowing angrily at anyone who disturbed him. It wasn't safe for Willa or me to live there anymore.

Their dad and I are friendly now, our two separate households of yesteryear evolving into our two actually separate households. Willa lives with me, and Diego with his dad.

I have been practicing law for five years and started my own firm before the pandemic. The firm is all women, and we represent parents in custody cases, some with kids struggling with truancy, depression, and drug use. Our clients are moms and dads struggling with each other, with themselves, and with their kids. They grieve the loss of what they had dreamed of being as parents, for the unexpected and unplanned changes to their lives and how things just didn't turn out how they had planned. "I've been there," I tell them. "You will get through it."

On some level, I know these parents are my younger self, and that my perceived shortcomings as a mother are why I devote myself so completely to guiding them now. Every parent who comes to my office seeking advice on custody, divorce, separation, or any of the myriad slings and arrows life throws at us is me, too.

Diego's profound need to have something outside himself (that piece of candy, that Lego, that phone, that car) meant that he was always on shifting sand—happy and content for a moment until he saw the next thing, just out of reach, that he wanted instead. Maybe that's how we all are, and that's what I did in becoming a lawyer. At last, I cherish what I now hold in my hands, this brass ring that I am gripping and holding onto for dear life.

Both children are grown now—Willa is almost seventeen. She is thriving, her quiet years behind her. She plays sports, has close friends, and loves school. She is interested in psychology and will be applying to colleges soon. Diego just turned eighteen and still lives at his dad's but doesn't go out much. He dipped his toe into high school last year but stopped going and has retreated into himself again. I invite him to do things, which he declines. If I come to visit, he doesn't take off his headphones or look away from the computer. I have had to accept that every heartfelt effort we all made to inspire and cajole him to participate in life and be loved just hasn't taken hold yet. But there's still time.

Diego is finally free, a legal adult not beholden to anyone or anything other than to the laws that govern the rest of us. I hold out hope every day that even though he is not required to love me or his dad and sister or anyone else, he will choose to anyway.

Abigail Seymour

Abigail C. Seymour is the founder and CEO of <u>Camino Law</u>, an all-female law firm in Greensboro, North Carolina, where she and four other attorneys practice family law, including surrogacy and grandparent custody as well as family-based immigration, including VAWA and SIJS. A second-career attorney, Abigail went to law school at forty-seven after a career as a photographer and journalist. She lived in Spain after college and speaks fluent Spanish. Abigail has been a speaker and podcast guest on the topic of reinvention, second careers, and healthy co-parenting.

Abigail is a Goldman Sachs 10,000 Small Businesses scholar and the recipient of an Empowering Women award from NC Lawyers Weekly for her approach to creating a non-traditional and mom-friendly law firm culture. She received her Bachelor's (BA) from New York University's Tisch School of the Arts, and her Juris Doctor (JD) from Elon University School of Law.

https://www.facebook.com/abigail.seymour

https://www.instagram.com/abigail_c_seymour

https://www.tiktok.com/404?fromUrl=/abogada_abigail

3

The Illusion of a Work-Life-Family Balance

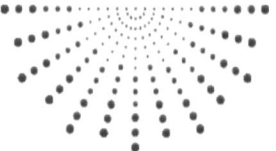

Amy Mitchell Pooley

T ears sprang to my eyes, and I felt the exhaustion of my seven months of pregnancy as we pulled a U-Haul up to the brick townhome. We had left our 18-month-old with a sitter in Austin. He was far too young to understand our task. My husband squeezed my hand knowing how hard today would be. "There's no rush."

Somehow my legs carried me to the front door and up the narrow stairs. The "Gralva" mug we had gifted him for Christmas was on display. The apartment-warming plant we delivered a couple of years earlier was flourishing. The rocking chair, the blankets, the big green couch...all exactly as I remembered. Everything in his apartment had a place. It was ordered. It was logical.

My home, on the other hand, brimmed with chaos—vivid and varied colors on every wall, piles of unread books, an ever-changing assortment of kid toys, and pet hair everywhere. His apartment was quiet, tidy, and impeccably clean. He was the type who would wipe the dining table while you were still eating and vacuum up invisible crumbs.

But a few things surprised me on this final visit.

His walk-in closet was full of designer clothes and at least a dozen pairs of Italian leather shoes. This from the man who rejected shirts with alligators on them for years.

The sheer volume of toiletries, mostly from the work trips he'd taken. *Is this why I collect lotion like it's going out of style?* A recent painting hanging on the wall with his name on it. I knew he was a once-upon-a-time art major, but I can't remember an artsy side to him. Instead, he worked his way up the corporate ladder at one of the largest telecommunications companies in the country, a path I later learned was designed to let him retire early as a millionaire so he could sit back and enjoy his later years.

It was obvious that he did not plan to leave us at 63.

One month earlier.

My cell phone rang. It was my mom, her voice shaking. "Hi, Ame. Are you at home right now?"

"No, I'm at a coffee house. I..."

I was terrified. At this point, my dad had been incommunicado for several days, and we had arranged for a well-check. "I'll call you when I get home."

Driving the three miles across town felt like it took an eternity. My mind was racing. Was he sick? Hurt? Drunk? In hermit mode?

I rushed into the house and beelined to my bedroom.

"Hi, Mom. I'm home."

I sat down on the chair next to the bed and held my breath.

"Your dad...uh, he died."

In the weeks and months following my father's death, my mind flashed with memories of him. Some memories were filtered through the lens of my younger self, when I didn't yet understand what it meant to be an adult or a parent, and others were through my grown-up lens, which helped me understand who he was and the choices he'd made.

"*Please* be quiet, Amy. Your dad's trying to sleep," my mom implored. It was seven-thirty at night, nineteen-eighty-something. My dad would invariably be up by five in the morning to get ready for work, something my own husband does now. Parent Amy appreciates that the wee hours of the morning are the easiest time to get some peace and quiet in a house with young children. Child Amy thought that my father must prefer being at work to being home. "Money doesn't grow on trees, Amy!" I heard for the millionth time. *I know, I know, you work hard. We never know what might happen. It's good to have a contingency plan. Don't live beyond your means...* Parent Amy can appreciate the sentiment way more than Child Amy ever did. My husband and I are constantly draining our bank accounts on seemingly endless baby items and renovations and repairs for our 1950s fixer-upper. My dad must have felt a ton of pressure to keep working to earn money for the family.

From time to time, the Clark Griswold version of my dad appeared, helped by the fact that my dad had the Chevy Chase chin dimple. I vividly remember my dad being chased by a family of raccoons on one of our many camping trips, cutting down the biggest tree at the Christmas tree farm, and taking on a playful "Bogeyman" persona. And it was the giddy Griswold version of my dad that hopped in the car at midnight to drive for three hours down I-35 when my husband called him to say that I was headed to the hospital to deliver his first grandchild. Parent Amy wondered what kind of memories her own kids would have of her as a mother. *Would they remember me more as a workaholic or a playmate?*

Less than four months after my father's death, my second child was born, a healthy baby boy. His heartbeat was strong, and, just like his brother, he was able to raise his head within hours of his birth. I affectionately called them my "turtle boys" for how they could lay on their tummies and raise their heads up with their strong little necks.

The very same day I gave birth, I officially landed the role of Chair of the Entertainment & Sports Law Section of the State Bar of Texas, the top position in the statewide Texas entertainment law organization. As a solo attorney with no background working in the larger markets of New York and California, it took a decade of scrappiness and hand-raising to earn the position. *Social chair? Sure! Website help? Me me me! Articles for the newsletter? I can help!*

It was exactly the type of professional accomplishment I would have loved to share with my dad. *Look, Dad! I am working my way up, too!* Instead, I was in a hospital bed, trying to figure out how to feed and soothe the newest member of the family. Why can't babies come with instruction manuals and off switches?

But flying blind was a familiar feeling for me. Unlike my younger brother, who knew what he wanted to do when he was a teenager and, in his words, "took the necessary steps to get there," I was much more of a meanderer. I changed majors, took odd jobs, and spent my meager income on traveling and collecting stories. So, when I announced, out of the blue, that I was going to law school based on eleven pages of a book written by a music lawyer, my family was dubious. After all, Lawyer and Free Spirit are not typically compatible.

I was, however, deeply committed to my goal of becoming a music lawyer. Where I had previously kept my eyes peeled for new paths, I now had a narrow ambition to represent musical talent. In many ways, life was easier than it had ever been. Having settled on one giant goal made it easier to choose classes and activities, as opposed to being a leaf in the wind. Unfortunately, my tunnel vision stumped my law school career counselors, and I bombed the few on-campus interviews I landed by focusing solely on how great it would be if ABC Law Firm created a music law division for me.

With no music law job materializing after graduation, I hung a shingle as a music lawyer the day that I passed the Texas bar exam. (Thanks to my dad always encouraging me to have a backup plan, I was enrolled in massage school at the time.) I took on my first client, a local band, within 24 hours. They needed a simple two-page contract reviewed prior to signing. Feeling the gravity of my first job as a bona fide music lawyer, I spent hours analyzing those words and charged them a whopping $75. To be clear, that's the kind of thing one can do when she has cheap rent and is only supporting herself and a cat. I do not recommend it as a long-term strategy, and I have steadily increased my legal fees over the course of my career.

By the time I had my second child, I had run my law firm as a true solo for twelve years—meaning that, in addition to doing the actual billable work, I handled all of the phone-answering, client intake, scheduling, billing, and marketing—and had a handful of sustaining production clients for which I did ongoing work. As a result, there was no easy "off switch" for my now busy practice. Without me, the firm simply could not run.

I did my best to give clients a heads up (pregnancy does not typically sneak up on a person), but, ultimately, I did what I'd done the first time around—I took a deep breath, set my email autoresponder to "Maternity Leave," and hoped for the best...while fretting about the worst. *What if my clients don't or can't wait for me? How long can I reasonably take to get back to work? What if my brain never feels normal again? (Mommy brain is real!)*

But this time around, my grief from losing my dad knocked me down on a daily basis, making it even harder to focus on anything. When I looked at my little ones, I was flooded with thoughts of how my dad would never have a chance to watch them grow up, teach them how to fish or play pool, share bad jokes, and give them bear hugs. When I wasn't tending to the baby, I was trying to triage my work emails, spend quality time with my husband and toddler, and take care of basic personal needs like eating and showering. Where I used to pride myself on drafting contracts and my attention to detail, I was sending documents out in despair, hoping they hung together because my eyes were too tired or tear-filled to read them again.

The truth is, most days, I felt like a failure as a professional, a wife, and a mom. That king-size bed with way too many pillows—right next to the chair where I'd received the worst news I could imagine—was inevitably where I spent any minutes that weren't claimed for breastfeeding or work calls.

Then, on a November night in 2016, my husband and I exchanged our champagne glasses for whiskey as we watched the political map on CNN in horror. *How was this possible? What kind of country are we living in? How can we raise kids here? Maybe they'd be too young to remember...*

The tumultuous political climate in the US was too much to process on top of a year that was already too much.

Getting out of bed became nearly impossible for the rest of the year. I was back to waking up in tears several times a night. I felt like some special breed of zombie who could still produce milk for her infant and manage to collect children from preschool and take the kiddos to a weekly music class.

But while most other moms at drop-off and pickup (*seriously, why do we moms do ninety percent of the child-transporting jobs?*) were excitedly chattering about their latest Pinterest boards and how they couldn't get enough snuggling and head-sniffing into each precious day as so-and-so's mom, I felt guilty plotting how I could arrange for even more time away from my kids to tackle the mountain of client work that had accumulated.

Was something wrong with me that I didn't miss my children every minute that I was away from them? If they didn't smell like the most delicious flower on the planet to my nose, was I a Bad Mom? Was it a total coincidence that the lead character in Bad Moms *was, in fact, named Amy Mitchell??*

By the time my second child was six months old, there was no escaping the need for extra childcare. But never in a million years did I think my family would hire a full-time nanny. Nannies were for rich people who couldn't be bothered to spend time with their own children. But I had no family nearby, an equally busy spouse who now worked in San Antonio three to four days per week, and an ever-increasing workload. So, when I learned that a nanny could help with drop-offs and pickups, caring for sick kids, working school holidays, shuttling kids to and from activities, preparing kid meals, doing laundry, and generally helping with tidying the house (i.e., all the things that were exhausting me), I was sold.

As it turned out, adding someone to our "home team" was exactly the boost my family needed. Suddenly, I had choices again as to how I spent my time. If my child was fussing or a meeting interfered with preschool pickup, I didn't have to reschedule the meeting or drop off the call. I also didn't have to worry about leaning more on my husband, who never hesitates to help when he can, even though he already has enough on his own plate to fill up several lifetimes. My husband and I even took some much-needed date nights once I realized that I didn't have to be home for every bedtime.

To be clear, I felt a bit awkward (and bougie) when I sent our nanny to preschool pickups. I still do. There's so much societal pressure on moms to show up for All The Things for their kids. However, lawyering and momming are both demanding jobs, and I am 1000% sure that I can't do either effectively if I'm running on empty. Scheduling "nanny hours" thus became synonymous with reclaiming some of the precious personal time that allowed me the space to build my law practice in the first place and to lead an adventure-filled adult life for fifteen years before becoming a mom.

Suffice it to say, raising kids takes a village and a nanny quickly became a key part of mine.

Fast forward another couple of years, and we welcomed our third child into the family, a baby girl. Unfortunately, with three kids under the age of five, day-to-day life tipped back to nearly unmanageable. No one was getting enough sleep, and tensions were high. I was back to working in one- to two-hour bursts and feeling like a failure on all fronts.

We weren't completely naïve. We knew having a third child would be hard. We'd be outnumbered. Plus, I had graduated from "advanced maternal age" to a full-on "geriatric pregnancy." But we felt that we were experienced enough now that we could manage it, especially when you factored in my husband's paternity leave (a luxury that we didn't have with our first two) and our long-term nanny.

We were wrong. Within a couple of months of becoming a family of five, our nanny unexpectedly put in her notice, and I felt like I was on the Titanic. I could hear my dad's voice in my head asking, "Well, what's your contingency plan, Ame?"

Mustering every ounce of energy, I created a job posting and started the time-consuming and frustrating task of finding and interviewing a new nanny. Turns out there are far fewer nannies willing to take a job caring for three young kids: infant, two, and four. We heard several variations on the theme of "sounds like you have your hands full" and "that's more care responsibilities than I am prepared to take on right now." *If professional nannies didn't have the energy for my kids 30-40 hours/week, what exactly am I supposed to do*?

But nothing prepared us for what was to come. On March 13, 2020, schools and businesses around the country shuttered, and my home became a fortress overnight. For weeks, my husband and I were glued to the news, trying to grasp the dangers of the novel coronavirus for our family of five. I started reading voraciously about epidemiology, which, if you know me at all, is not the literature you would expect to see on my shelf.

For me, the mental taxation of the early pandemic (*How are we supposed to stop our young kids from touching things? Did you remember to spray bleach on the bags before you brought them? Do we have enough toilet paper? Diapers? How many days has the mail been outside? Can I touch my face yet? How the hell do we take all of these preventative steps without freaking out the kids?*) was different than the newborn days. The newborn phase is defined. It's Google-able (though I typically tell new moms to resist the urge to Google every little thing). Suddenly, that age-old adage of "this, too, shall pass" no longer seemed reliable. We had no idea how long we would be unwilling shut-ins or have our kids learn and interact with teachers and peers solely through the wonders of the internet. Would it be weeks? Months? Years? We were navigating uncharted parenting waters. I doubted that my father would have had a contingency plan for "global pandemic hits while parenting young children."

By late 2020, we had cobbled together a very small village. However, going against the current in the south, we remained mostly closed off for another two years. "Damn liberals," I imagined strangers thinking when they saw our family of five pile out of the minivan and dutifully put on our masks before walking through the door.

I didn't care. Protecting my family from the possibility of a life cut short (either theirs or the life of a loved one) was too important for me to consider letting down my guard. I didn't wish my painful experience of grieving the sudden loss of a loved one on anyone.

On December 1, 2022, my daughter and I exited the clinic on a cold and rainy day, and I fully exhaled for the first time in years. I felt my shoulders drop several inches from their semi-permanent residence up near my ears. She had a fresh bandaid on her upper arm, a moment my husband and I had been anxiously awaiting for nearly three years. I teared up. FINALLY! We could take off the masks. We could say yes to seeing family, even the anti-vaxxers. We could plan trips and let the kids show their full faces at school. We could finally live in the open again. It was exhilarating.

Within months, the kids were signed up for swim lessons, gymnastics, math club, karate, Minecraft club, and more. Where I had seen my kids morning, noon, and night for years, I suddenly saw them only for a brief time before and after school. Now, I had "me time" in spades, but, to my surprise, I missed the (forced) together time and perceived lack of choice about where and how to spend my time. *Was I actually a **better** mom thanks to the pandemic? Had we overcorrected? What kind of relationship would I have with my kids now that I could return to work as usual? **Should** I return to work as usual? What does "usual" even mean to someone like me?*

So, after a multi-year hiatus, I returned to the daunting task of prioritizing how I would balance my time between work and family.

First, I created a colorful family calendar. My husband had committed to doing the various school drop-offs before he left for work, so I focused on the two or three different school pickups and near-daily swim classes (not letting my kids drown was also high on my priority list). Putting everything in writing was a wake-up call. If I actually handled all of the afternoon people-moving, I would only have a mere three to four hours per day to work, eat, and take care of my own personal things.

What could I outsource?

Honestly, I didn't relish outsourcing school pickups. I **love** school pickup! Big smiles, hugs, and a few minutes of happy chatter on the walk or drive home? Yes, please! It also gives me a chance to stretch my legs and clear my head. Win-win-win. Plus, I had read that school pickup was one of those critical times for kids to have consistency in their daily routines. I was, however, perfectly fine to outsource getting kids to and from swim class and other activities that required wrangling gear and/or snacks.

Could I simply work less?

After adding up the cost of preschool, after-school clubs, swim lessons, extra childcare, etc., and reminding myself of the damage done by my retail therapy that spiraled after my dad's death,

I realized that I needed to earn at least as much as I had been bringing in, not less. *I am determined to live within my means, Dad. I promise.*

How could I work smarter?

This is where being your own boss can be a blessing. In addition to immediately bumping up my hourly rate (most women need to do this!), I took a hard look at my "systems." I wrote down the type of work that I enjoyed doing and that generated the best revenue. Then, I updated my law firm website to better reflect those focus areas and fees and created online scheduling links and intake forms that automated what used to take multiple emails. I also cut out free consultations. As one of the most experienced entertainment attorneys in Austin at this point, I could have filled all twenty-six hours per week on free consultations.

Most importantly, I committed to only taking on work that interested me and that I felt I could reasonably do in the hours of the day that I was willing and able to devote to work, which, after extensive soul-searching, I had decided was four days a week from 9:30 a.m. - 4:00 p.m. The fifth weekday I would reserve for my personal appointments and special projects. I added these limited working hours to my signature block and legal representation agreement, with a note that any work required on an expedited basis outside of those "regular work hours" was not guaranteed and may be subject to an "after-hours" surcharge (*if plumbers charge more after hours, why can't lawyers?*).

Knowing that most lawyers work far more than twenty-six hours per week, I was both anxious and exhilarated to have established such strong client boundaries. *But would I stick to them and follow through on my goals to commit those other hours to myself and my family? Could I escape my workaholic DNA to be the kind of mom that I want to be?*

More than one year later, I continue to struggle mightily to take off my lawyer hat on nights and weekends. Writing down boundaries and goals is far easier than maintaining and achieving them. For me, putting limited working hours in my signature block is the easy part. But actually pausing my draft response to a work email to play with my kiddo at three-thirty on a Saturday is hard. At the same time, I've fully accepted that I won't be the Pinterest mom who wears Lululemon and volunteers for every school event: I need space to be a lawyer, too.

I also don't expect there to be some magical moment when everything feels perfectly in balance between my lawyer and mom roles. True work-life-family balance is an illusion. It's more about avoiding obvious imbalances—when something (or someone) important is getting neglected or taking over. Plus, if the last ten years have taught me anything, it's that the unexpected will happen, and I need to be prepared to reassess and pivot.

What I am fighting so hard for is to feel at peace with how I invest my time in my career, in my family, and in myself since I know that time is not guaranteed to any of us. Working my butt off for thirty years is no guarantee that I will get to sit back and enjoy the next thirty. If I'm lucky enough to have a lot of tomorrows, it would break my heart to look back and realize that I missed truly experiencing my children growing up by doom-scrolling or blindly escaping into work or trying to earn a few more bucks or credits for my IMDb page. So, I owe it to my future heart to put away the devices and be fully present with my kids as much as possible. Plus, my children deserve a mom who prioritizes true togetherness and personal connection over connection to the internet. My most fervent wish is to fill my children's buckets with laughter, dance parties, family hugs, silly songs, and adventures by land and sea because, at the end of the road, the "Griswold" moments matter most.

Amy Mitchell Pooley

Austinite Amy Mitchell Pooley is the founding member of the entertainment law boutique firm <u>Amy E Mitchell, PLLC</u>, which primarily serves creative professionals in the music, film, and television industries. Amy is also a creative in her own right and performs as a vocalist, keyboardist, and occasional ukulele player.

Drawing from her lifetime of experiences as a performer and twenty years as a solopreneur, Amy frequently advises other attorneys and creatives on how to navigate and build a career in the entertainment industry. In fact, her strong desire to educate, guide, and protect creatives from doing bad deals and lawyers from doing legal jobs they hate has inspired The Entertainment Law Mama project, which officially launches in 2024. However, loving on her three children will always be her #1 "mama" gig. Amy earned both her B.A. (1999) and J.D. (2004) from the University of Texas at Austin.

https://www.linkedin.com/in/Austinentertainmentlawyer

https://www.instagram.com/entertainmentlawmama/

https://www.facebook.com/entertainmentlawmama

4

Joyful Sobriety

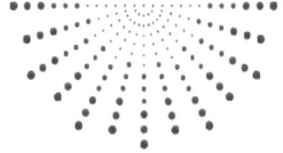

Kate Lincoln-Goldfinch

It was pitch black in the middle of the night. I was driving down a long stretch of two-lane highway, heading home after a long shift of cocktail waitressing at a popular club on Sixth Street in downtown Austin. My friend sat in the passenger seat as I tested the limits of her mom's brand-new Nissan Altima. We had a cooler full of Zimas in the trunk and no cares in the world. It was our last year in high school.

It was a zippy little car, and I wanted to see how fast we could go. I pressed the pedal. For several minutes, we topped out at over 100 mph. Then, the two-lane highway merged. I slammed the brakes to avoid hitting a horse trailer that appeared out of nowhere in the lane next to me. We spun around several times and came to a stop just a foot away from the concrete median.

As I collected myself, I looked over at my friend. She was as wide-eyed as I was. I took a deep breath and began to get back on the road. That's when I felt the grind of metal on asphalt. Lost in the thrill of going too fast, the tires exploded. So I pulled over.

The police had been following us. The officer issued me a speeding ticket. I remember the date because it was the night Lady Diana died in a car crash: August 31, 1997. Although I'd gotten lucky in so many ways, I never drove under the influence again.

That's not to say I completely abandoned my wild ways. After graduating high school, dropping out of college, and securing a corporate job, I lived in an apartment on Sixth Street. More nights than not, I went out drinking and partying. Rinse and repeat. After hosting after-hours parties, I would show up at work hungover. I kept fans on my desk to cool me down and save me from hangover nausea.

Ironically, I only toned things down when I reentered college at the University of Texas. Despite the school's reputation as a party hotbed, I curbed my drinking when I joined the rowing team. I took the sport seriously. The night before a home race, one of my boatmates stayed up all night drinking, and came late to the meet. We did not perform well.

After our loss, she told us about her epic night out. I was furious and snitched to the coach so she would get in trouble. While I cringe about it now, I felt so righteous in the moment. Though

I never lost that sense of morality and justice, I would bend the rules just a bit to justify my own drinking or while in the act thereof.

By my mid-twenties, I had married, bought a house, and started law school—all within two months. I'd also settled into my "adult" relationship with alcohol.

Lawyers are notoriously heavy drinkers, and more often than not, our indulgence begins as 1Ls. UT Law is a lot like high school, only the students are slightly older. There are a lot of parties, and drinking is an acceptable part of the culture. (At least, it was twenty years ago—who knows what it's like now.)

Besides finding my way to the bottom of more than a few bottles, I found something else as a law student: a calling, and a heavy one, at that. I'd narrowed my career focus and knew I wanted to work in social justice.

As an undergrad, I majored in political communication and worked with a Democratic campaign consultant. During law school, I gravitated toward politics or something in the public interest. I took internships at the Texas Capitol and at a nonprofit serving domestic violence victims. They were both fascinating and fulfilling placements but not yet the lifelong passion I had been hoping to find. I tried the immigration clinic at the law school because I wanted to use my Spanish, and it had a great reputation among students. It was there that I finally found my enduring spark.

My first assignment was to conduct an intake at a family detention center for asylum seekers. The family I worked with was from Iraq—a mother, a father, and a five-month-old baby girl. All three were clad in prison-issued clothing; I'll never forget the baby and her navy blue prison onesie. During that meeting, the mother asked me if I would hold her baby because I smelled like the outside world. As we finished, the mother asked if I would take her baby and care for her until she and her husband could get out.

I can't tell you what I'd lost in that moment—naivete, innocence, optimism, hope, it's too squishy a word—but I was crestfallen. I'd thought the United States was a land of immigrants. That we are who we claim to be on the Statue of Liberty. On assignment one, I was saddled with the painful reality of our immigration laws.

That case at least closed on a hopeful note—as a law student, I won their asylum hearing. I picked them up from detention and took them shopping at Target for new clothes on their way to the airport.

I was hooked. I stayed in the clinic for the rest of my time in law school, representing clients in asylum hearings. The more I studied and explored, the more convinced I became that I had found something I could spend my career doing. Give me your tired, your poor, and your huddled masses yearning to breathe free. All of them.

After graduating from law school, I obtained a fellowship to work with detained families seeking asylum for two years. I carried the entire weight of my work on my shoulders back then—I even had terrible back troubles to prove it. I used alcohol to numb and to escape—to unburden myself from the heaviness of my work. After long full days at the detention center talking to hundreds of desperate people, and only being able to help a handful because of capacity constraints, I would drive home and dream about my first drink. It was the first thing I did as I walked in the door. Many nights, if not most nights, I would drink enough to be fuzzy. I welcomed the feeling.

Yet every joyous night has its morning after, and I can't say I was able to connect the daily morning dread to the drinking until much later and after many more nights. The doom felt normal—doesn't *everyone* wake up this way? With their minds racing, their hearts pounding, and their scattershot attempts to piece together their yesterdays and work through what must be done today?

In the beginning, I wanted to heal my clients *and* get their legal status in order. Naturally, I burned out eighteen months into my fellowship. The back pain. The overwhelming need. The coping. Despite how much I cared, I remember thinking I had chosen the wrong profession. It was all so heavy; it was all too much. And that was *before* I went into private immigration practice and learned how to do the rest of the work required for my profession.

I was weary and wary, so I called my mom. She gave me brilliant advice, telling me my responsibility is "limited to the tiny sliver of time in which I interact with my clients." I can't fix their before; I can't fix their after. I can't erase and heal what's been done, but I can do the best I can while I'm working with them.

That reminder was freeing. I decided to set down some of the responsibility for what my clients had gone through. I still worked on detained asylum cases, but it was not one hundred percent of my job anymore. I also got to do other court cases, help clients receive and renew green cards, and obtain crime victims' visas. I welcomed the variety, and the challenges inspired me.

As I settled into my career, I also got pregnant with my first baby, Norie, and quelled my drinking for the second time in my life. I didn't drink during pregnancy or while on maternity leave, but upon returning to work, the weight became too much and the drinking resumed. Life to that point never gave me a real break. With more to do at work and a tiny human to raise at home, I needed to escape more than ever. I think of the Calgon commercial ("Take me away!") and all the noises that weigh on a woman melting away in the tub. For me, I found my quiet in a few glasses of wine. I learned about pumping and dumping when I wanted to drink and got back to my routine of escaping it all with some alcohol at night.

Motherhood and lawyering weigh on you. Over the next eight years, that weight became crushing. I had another baby and opened my law firm. Both the child and the firm grew fast. Before I knew it, I had two kids, dozens of employees, and hundreds of clients counting on me—and it's not like the immigration landscape got simpler or quieter.

President Obama ended family detention—the policy that allowed my first family's infant to be outfitted in a prison onesie—in 2014. Just before leaving office, he brought the policy back. Things at the border were heating up, and the US had opened two giant detention centers for families in Central Texas. I had a client in one of those jails—a little girl with a brain tumor whose condition was worsening. The facility would not release her or let her out. To get her out, I ended up having to go to the media.

The stress and time in the public eye were uncomfortable, yet that discomfort paled in comparison to the way the job evolved after Trump took office. Any immigration lawyer who worked during those four years understands the drive to drink. At one point, his administration issued or changed US immigration and customs policies every four days. It was nonstop. Our clients were panicked, and rightly so. To make matters much, much worse, the way we treated migrants deteriorated to crisis levels. As we learned more about the horrors at the border, new atrocities kept coming. The conditions in the camps were unnerving, yet that was nothing compared to the way we separated kids from their families.

When we first received word of family separations back in June 2018, I got called to the same detention center where I had started my career in immigration law. That summer day was a lot like my first day there, so many years before. It was as bad as you would imagine.

I encountered women whose children were taken from them. Upon arrival in the US, they had their children ripped from their arms by Border Patrol officers. The mothers I spoke with were asylum seekers who had fled horrific situations with their young children and were just focused on one thing: getting those kids to safety. They were sent to the detention center alone, and by the time I met with them, it had been weeks without information on their children. Where were they? When would they see them again? No one could say.

I felt absolute shock and horror that this was even possible—as did most of us who were paying attention. These women needed the most urgent help, and none of the local nonprofits could help reunite them with their kids.

I worked that summer to reunite about forty mothers with their children. As the summer dragged on, the Border Patrol officers got more clever and nefarious in their methods. They started tricking moms into releasing their kids for temporary processing or to have a photo taken in the next room, and then the children would be taken. It was devastating.

In one particular case, Trump himself defied a court order to release my client. I appeared on Rachel Maddow's show that night to talk about it, in the hopes it might make a difference in her case. I felt the pressure and weight of it all. My kids—ages six and one then—were all I could see in every client I helped that summer. I drank most nights throughout that experience. It just felt like the horror would never end or even ease.

And then, Covid happened. My anxiety, already through the roof, reached new skyscraping heights. How would I serve my clients, continue daily operations, and keep my business afloat? Would we catch Covid? Would my parents be okay? Why must my kiddo hate Zoom school? (In retrospect, who didn't hate Zoom school?) I drank daily. At first, to self-medicate, but later just because it was routine. What else was there to do? In addition to being scared to death, weren't we all just so…bored?

That's when my drinking finally affected my family. Not my marriage—my husband and I drank together and encouraged each other to have a drink when we wanted one. We had fun. We were not drunk fighters, and most of the time, it worked for us to drink together, but we did not encourage each other to make wise choices. I started drinking in front of my kids. Although most of my fuzzy moments were after they were asleep, I relaxed protocol on holidays and weekends.

Vacations required constant drinking. I felt an urgent need to hurry up and relax, and the only way I knew how was to drink. I'd spend the whole day on the beach, drinking alcohol. By the time we'd get back to our lodging, I'd be too tired to cook or do anything and just fall asleep—you might call it "passing out."

On weekends at home, I would sometimes start drinking while the sun was still shining and not finish until close to the kids' bedtime.

I remember one of the last times I drank. Norie was eight, and we had some friends over to hang out in our backyard, so the kids stayed up late. I was drunk enough to slur my words, but didn't know it until I was speaking and looked over at Norie, who was sitting next to me in a camping chair. I could see her perplexed look. My words were coming out funny. I remember feeling a lot of shame at that moment and thinking, "Uh oh, my kid is old enough to have memories of me being drunk now."

All my life, I'd been what I call a "gray area" drinker. I vacillated between destructive and harmless drinking. I didn't have a dramatic rock bottom moment. Over time, the haze formed a cloud, and it was all just gray. Life didn't get dark; the color just disappeared. I used alcohol primarily as a treat to reward myself for doing hard things. I also used it to escape, to combat boredom and anxiety, and to make myself more interesting—or so I thought. If you've ever been the sober one in a room full of drunks, you are painfully aware of how uninteresting they all are. As it turns out, there are a lot of us.

Boy howdy, did I need something to snap me out of my daily drinking habit. I felt puffy, yucky, and more than just a little bit stuck. Six months into the pandemic, a friend invited me to do an alcohol detox with her. An online group called Sober Sis had a guided 21-day program that would end right before the holidays. In my mind, I was thinking, "I can do this and still have fun for the holidays." So, I signed up for the program and started getting the daily emails. Each one profoundly spoke to me—and they were just emails. I learned how to handle cravings, holidays, events, anxiety and stress, and was able to answer questions like...what if my spouse is still drinking, did I really drink for taste, how does the liquor industry market to women, what is gray-area drinking, can I drink in moderation, and what comes next? Each day's subject line and email was just the stepping stone I needed.

During the detox, I also read books by sober women. They were inspiring. The first book I read was *Quit Like a Woman* by Holly Whitaker. In her book, Whitaker outlines how the alcohol industry is (mostly) controlled by only fourteen massive companies. This cartel has spent just as much as the tobacco industry in convincing us that alcohol is a healthy and normal part of celebrations, rituals, society, and adulthood. Another book I loved was *The Unexpected Joy of Being Sober* by Catherine Gray.

Catherine really challenges the idea that sober life is boring, and she gave me hope for a brighter future without alcohol.

As my detox wound down, I began to contemplate my relationship with alcohol on a more permanent level. I took inventory of my life in the three weeks without drinking. When I looked in the mirror, my skin was more luminous. My clothes fit without pinching. I was rested and hadn't woken up at three in the morning with my mind racing in weeks. I did not wake up with a sense of impending doom. I had no regrets about my behavior or my actions, no cringe moments about that thing I said or did when I was drunk. I was a better mom and a better wife. I was kinder to myself. Everywhere I looked, life had improved. I could feel a weight slowly start to lift.

Sober Sis opened my eyes to a burgeoning sober-curious movement. As I continued to think about how I wanted my relationship with alcohol to evolve, I decided to wait to drink again until I gained more clarity...maybe two weeks?

Famous last words. Two weeks turned into two months turned into two years. In the first month after I stopped drinking, my husband joined me on this journey. He had joined the law firm, and we were growing and raising our family and our business together. Together, we are not perfect or sunshine or rainbows—but most days, we are thriving.

As I write this chapter, I am in the midst of some real professional challenges. Our kids have struggled with post-pandemic academic and social life, and we have had to be focused parents and business owners. I feel crippling anxiety often, but it's not the characteristic dread-based *hangxiety* coupled with shame that's a hallmark of too much drink and not enough growth. The world is more clear. The weight of everything is more manageable.

I just celebrated my third sober anniversary. I'd hazard a guess that there's never been a better time to be a sober-curious person. The binary of "alcoholics get sober while everyone else drinks" is reductive and not how sobriety works in 2024. Nearly every function now offers mocktails, and most women can decline alcohol without everyone wondering if she's pregnant—and, yes, I remember pretending to drink alcohol at functions when I was newly and privately pregnant with Norie—or in a twelve-step program.

I think about the way things become heavier and less colorful the deeper you drag them below the surface. Objects look less bright and more blue the deeper they are underwater (in the absence of an artificial light source). In many ways, the color drained from my life as the haze arrived and the pressure got at me. I wasn't drinking so much as I was drowning. Perhaps I was the weight I was lifting. As I've risen to the surface, I see brighter, bolder, and clearer colors before me.

Kate Lincoln-Goldfinch

K ate Lincoln-Goldfinch is an advocate, mother, wife, and immigration attorney from Austin, Texas. In 2015, Kate founded Lincoln-Goldfinch Law, an award-winning immigration and bankruptcy law firm. Lincoln-Goldfinch Law has served thousands of families who are searching for peace of mind and a fresh start.

A recognized authority in immigration matters, she has appeared as an expert on renowned news platforms including NBC, BBC, MSNBC, *The New York Times*, Fox News, and National Public Radio.

Originally from Austin, Kate attended UT Law School with dreams of positively impacting her community. Kate's proudest accomplishment of all is raising her children together with her husband Josh to be thoughtful, socially aware activists who will leave the world a better place.

https://www.instagram.com/katelincolngoldfinch/

https://www.instagram.com/lincolngoldfinchlaw/

https://www.linkedin.com/in/lincolngoldfinch/

https://www.linkedin.com/company/lincoln-goldfinch-law/

https://www.tiktok.com/@attorneyklg

https://www.facebook.com/lincolngoldfinch

5
Three New Hats

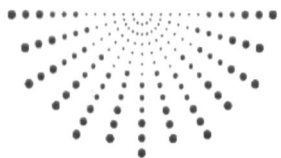

Caitlin Haney Johnston

I attended law school twice, once in vitro and the other when I was twenty-two years old. Already the mother of two children, my mom decided to go to law school when my brother was old enough to be in school full-time. An "oops baby," I was born the day after her last final during the fall semester of her 3L year. Her greatest fear was that she would go into labor during the test and no one would help her. Luckily, I understood the assignment and stayed put.

As a child, I learned a lot from watching her career. Most importantly, I learned that you will lose sometimes, but you have to keep going. She loved to say the only lawyers who have never lost a case are the ones who don't take hard cases. She also taught me to keep my eye on the end result, be it a trial, a test, or a paper that was due. Once that was finished, you dealt with the other stuff.

Mom was always there—chaperoning field trips, attending school recitals, or hauling me to a horse show. Somehow, her being a lawyer made her schedule more flexible, even when she was working with a firm. She ran for judge when I was in middle school, and that was an experience of its own. Since she was divorced from my father, I often had to accompany her to caucus meetings and networking events. While she lost in the primary, I was so proud of her for seeing it through to the end. It was an extremely close race; she was ahead until the last few ballot boxes were counted.

After she lost the race, Mom knew she needed to do something different. She started her own law firm in 2001. A couple of years later, my sister, Amber, joined her as her paralegal. I joined her firm when I graduated from law school in 2013.

Working with my mother meant that I had a mentor who truly believed in me and wanted me to succeed. She pushed me to take depositions, lead hearings, and even first chair a jury trial two-and-a-half years into being a lawyer.

But it wasn't always easy. After first joining the firm, there was tension between all of us: my sister, who at that point had been my mom's paralegal for over ten years; my mom, dealing with a pretentious first-year lawyer who in some ways thought she was too good to be there; and me, somehow back where she started when I'd left eight years prior. Later on, disagreements would pop up over which cases to take and how much control over the business management she was willing to give up. But over time, despite some challenges, we figured out how to work together successfully. My mother loved to refer to us as the Haney Legal Dream Team.

In June of 2020, three months into the Covid pandemic, my sister called. Mom wasn't answering her phone.

I called Mom, and she sounded a little weird, but I thought maybe she was shaking off her sleeping medicine as it was still early in the morning on a Saturday. But then Mom kept texting weird things to our group chat, and after my sister finally got access to her home, we knew something was very, very off. The decision was made that she needed to go to the hospital, so I jumped in the car and started driving.

My sister accompanied Mom to the ER, where she was only allowed in because Mom wasn't making any sense. I parked in the parking lot outside and waited.

A text message from my sister:

"Taking her back for a CT scan now. They think it might be a stroke."

And then, thirty minutes later:

"No Stroke."

"Brain Tumor."

I will never forget this moment. Unable to speak, a primal scream escaped my body.

I knew what this meant. In 2014, two days after I turned twenty-seven, I was diagnosed with a very rare form of appendix cancer that we caught by sheer dumb luck. Indebted to the universe, I threw myself into the cancer community and co-founded a pro bono estate planning cancer clinic. That led to speaking at all types of cancer support groups, working with hospice workers, and even serving on a young adult cancer advisory board.

So I knew. A tumor in the brain typically meant one of two things: primal brain cancer or metastasized cancer. Neither had good outcomes.

And then it hit me—what in the hell am I going to tell our clients?

After a few essential phone calls to family and very close friends, I knew who had to be next. Celeste, our other paralegal. I never called her on a Saturday, so she answered on the first ring.

"Celeste, I have bad news. Susan is in the hospital—she has a brain tumor. She has to have brain surgery in two days."

I paused, took a breath, and continued, "Tomorrow, I am going to tell her active litigation cases that she will be out for at least six months. I will do what I need to in order to protect their cases, but they will need to decide if I am going to take over or if they want to hire outside counsel."

Another gasp of air, and I continued, "On Monday morning, I need you to file emergency medical leave letters in all of our litigation cases. Just use a vacation letter as a template. Make it for two weeks."

I don't remember exactly what Celeste said, but I know it was a mix of concern about Mom and knowing how important it was to get these things done.

The next morning, I called the clients in the cases Mom was handling. I needed to tell them before the emergency letters made it to opposing counsel what was going on. She had half a dozen or so active cases at that time, in various stages of litigation: One post-arbitration brief due in a few days, another headed to mediation in two weeks, and another awaiting a summary judgment ruling. I worked in each of them, but Susan did most of the heavy lifting.

For the most part, the clients were understanding.

For the most part.

I got to see Mom the following day. Apparently, when they plan to crack open your head and dig out a tumor, they think you should be allowed to see all three of your children, Covid restrictions or not.

I was sitting next to Mom, talking about cases and the business—she wanted to tell me what she thought needed to be done. She largely agreed with the steps we were taking and the game plan for the next couple of weeks. As crazy as it sounds now, there was a part of us at that point that thought this just might knock Mom out for several months, but she would be able to return to work.

Right before I was about to leave, the social worker came in. She talked to us about Mom's living situation, power of attorney, and her support system. As she was wrapping up, she got up and walked to the door. When Mom could no longer see her, she mouthed to me to come outside. I told Mom I needed to use the restroom and stepped out.

"I get the idea that no one has told you what this really means for your mom."

I looked at her, not knowing what she meant.

"She isn't going to be able to live alone ever again, much less work. She is never going to be able to do those things independently. You all should be preparing for that."

Bewildered, I said, "You don't know that."

And then she gave me the look. The look that said you're right, she didn't, but if this case followed the track that every other case she has seen does, that is the way it will end. It's probably the same face I make when I am talking to someone on the phone and I know that their case doesn't stand a chance.

Once she turned and walked away, I walked even further down the hall and called my sister.

"They said Mom will never be able to work again, or probably even live alone ever again." After rehashing all the information just dumped on me by the social worker, Amber and I both sat with it for a little bit. Then, "I don't think that will happen with Mom. She's too strong and stubborn." Amber agreed.

We also agreed that, in the meantime, I would ensure the business ran smoothly (so that all the cases were taken care of and she could come back on a part-time basis), and Amber would look for a home where they could live together (so that she could help and spend time with Amber's baby).

The day of Mom's surgery, we held vigil at her home. It was just my siblings, our spouses, and my niece and nephews. The surgery took at least eight hours, and they occasionally called with updates and let us know she was doing ok. Overall, the surgeon was happy—he was able to remove all of the tumor. However, he also had bad news for us—he was pretty sure that, based on the tumor's characteristics, it was a high-grade glioblastoma.

My brother, Ben, managed to speak, "What is the prognosis for that?"

A pause.

"Less than two years."

Pathology would confirm it was, in fact, glioblastoma. Not only that, but after genetic testing, we learned that it was an especially aggressive form of an especially aggressive brain cancer. We were told that the first step was for her to complete the standard of care—six weeks of daily chemotherapy and radiation once she recovered from the surgery.

Mom never took well to being told she needed to take it easy. Two days after her brain surgery, she tried responding to client emails on her phone—causing her to have seizures. We removed her phone from her until her brain healed from the trauma of surgery. She still insisted on being kept in the loop on the cases.

The first rounds of treatment weren't so bad. She would get a two-week break, then we enrolled her in a clinical trial at MD Anderson. We were told this particular drug, VAL083, would likely keep her tumor at bay for a year or so. All we had to do was drive Mom the three hours to MD Anderson every other week for three days of treatment.

No big deal for two sisters trying to keep a law firm running. One, the mother of an infant; the other, me, trying to get pregnant.

When Mom got sick, I immediately felt the need to try and have a child. We got pregnant the first cycle we tried but miscarried at seven weeks—not even enough time to tell much of my family or friends. I originally intended to keep it a secret from Mom, not wanting to add anything to her plate, but eventually, it came out.

It was now December 2020, and Covid was rampant. My sister ended up catching it and passing it to her almost one-year-old. Miraculously, even though Mom lived with Amber, she didn't catch it. But that meant that Mom needed to live with me until her follow-up at MD Anderson.

Despite everything else going on, we still had a business to run and clients to serve. I needed to drive to the office one day to check mail and write paychecks for everyone. Mom insisted on coming with me, even though I desperately wanted a break. On the way home, I tried talking to Mom about long-term plans for the firm.

I brought up the fact that at some point, I would (hopefully) need to plan for maternity leave, and that means saving up enough to keep the firm operational and hire *of counsel* folks to handle emergencies that popped up.

She insisted she could do it.

"Mom, you have a brain tumor that could grow back at any time; why do you think that is practical?"

Through gritted teeth, she responded, "Because nothing has ever stopped me before."

A week later, Amber (now recovered from Covid) took Mom to MD Anderson for an MRI and infusion of VAL083. We weren't expecting anything crazy—Mom had been doing pretty well overall, and they said most patients saw at least six to nine months of containment on the drug. After nine months the prognosis wasn't as good, but we were only three months in.

The MRI showed that the tumor was already growing back, so she was kicked out of the clinical trial. We spent the next week researching all of the other clinical trials available nationwide and speaking with consultants about her best options.

We enrolled our mother in a Stage 1 clinical trial—a Hail Mary—to see if we could steal some time for her. Not long after that, I learned I was pregnant, this time with a baby girl.

In May 2021, when I was four months pregnant, Mom was staying at our house to give my sister a small amount of respite. At this point, her verbal skills were significantly impaired, and she couldn't move around without assistance. I went into her room and started talking to her.

"Mom, it's time to get up and go to the bathroom."

Not immediately responsive, I went to help her sit up. At this point, it wasn't unusual for her to need assistance standing up, so I slipped my hands under her arms to steady her, but when she stood up, it felt like she was gumby—her legs were liquid. I tried keeping her steady, using what strength I had to keep us both up and rested against the wall. Then she started moving, and I was hopeful that this was her body fighting to get control.

But the shaking got worse, and I realized we were both going down. I screamed for my husband.

"Drew! Mom's having a seizure."

I tried my best to protect my small but growing pregnant belly while also trying to steady my mother, but I was incredibly relieved when he came into the room. He helped me lower her gently to the floor while we called 911. The seizure was thankfully short-lived, but still terrifying to watch.

Not long after that, Mom went into hospice care eleven months after her initial diagnosis. We fast-tracked my baby shower so that Mom could attend. My OB let us borrow a doppler from her office for the weekend so that my mom could at least hear the baby's heartbeat, since it was becoming clear she wouldn't meet my baby.

Now, in August 2021, our family and our firm were pushed to the limit. I was driving to work on I-35 when I started feeling light-headed. In the middle of rush hour traffic, I tried maneuvering off of the highway and made it to the exit ramp before I lost consciousness. After my car hit a curb, I regained consciousness in time to see a woman running to my window.

"Do you need an ambulance?"

"Yes, I am seven months pregnant. What happened?"

"You drove through the gas station."

"Did I hit anything?"

She laughed, "Um, yes. Several things."

Now, I was panicked, "Did I hurt anyone?"

She understood my concern, "No, no one was hit, just a light pole."

Luckily, after being checked out by the EMTs and my OB, we determined that everyone, including the baby, was fine. However, I received instructions to refrain from driving the rest of the pregnancy—so this meant that I had to rely on my husband to drive me to work and Ubers and friends to drive me around town.

On August 7, Mom celebrated her last birthday at the age of sixty-six.

August 11, hospice told us Mom's last day was upon us. With a hearing the next morning, I reached out to an attorney who previously agreed to handle some uncontested cases while I was on maternity leave (remember, at this point, I am almost eight months pregnant). She immediately agreed to handle my hearing so I could be with my family.

I called the court staff attorney. At this point, everyone knew Mom was sick, most people knew I was pregnant, and most people also knew that she hadn't been responsive in several days. The staff attorney assured me it would all be handled, and not to give it any more thought.

If you've ever waited for someone to die, you know it is a strange experience. Unlike typical situations, like a wedding or the birth of a baby, you aren't waiting for something joyful. You are both hoping it will happen soon to put her at peace while also begging the universe to pull out a miracle.

Around six o'clock in the evening on August 12, I went into my mother's room—it was my turn to stay with her and let her know we were there whenever she was ready to go.

I held her hand and petted her dog before lying down on the floor. Just as I got comfortable, the dog started whining and tried jumping off the hospital bed.

I immediately knew. She was gone.

As backward as it sounds, I was actually relieved. Not because I didn't miss my mother, but because now I knew she was out of pain. I felt like once her spirit was released from her body, I would have a better opportunity to connect with her.

I went over to the door and called my sister's name. As soon as her eyes met mine, she knew as well. I didn't have to say a word.

We shut down the office for a week or so, but with a baby coming in six weeks, there was only so much time I could take off.

Six weeks after my mother died, it was time for me to give birth to my own baby girl. I did the best I could to make sure my office would run smoothly for the four weeks I planned to take off. We filed vacation letters and told new clients who came in the last few weeks that their cases and documents would be delayed, giving them the opportunity to work with someone else if they desired. Via email, I gave clients a heads up I would be out and introduced them to the amazing attorneys who agreed to help out on an "of counsel" basis. To reduce administrative tasks, all bills eligible for autopay were put on autopay. In the months before maternity leave, money was saved and set aside to deal with the fact that I anticipated a twenty thousand dollar a month deficit between what we would bring in and our monthly expenses for at least two months. It was a long way from perfect, but the best I could do under the circumstances.

Like the preceding fourteen months, the delivery wasn't easy. Since she was premature, my daughter went to the NICU. My blood pressure kept dropping to almost nothing, so they ended up calling code on me. I asked one of the labor nurses, "Am I dying?"

"You are where you need to be." Not exactly comforting.

They transferred me down to the ICU, where I once again asked if I was dying. The ICU doctor laughed—"No, you are conscious, which makes you the healthiest person down here."

Oddly, that actually reassured me. My OB, who was technically off for the day, came back to the hospital and refused to leave. She was convinced I had to be hemorrhaging, but the ICU doctor thought if that was happening, I would say I was in more pain than I was. She told him, "You don't know her pain tolerance." She put me back under to take a look, and, sure enough, there was fluid buildup.

The following day, after a long night following the additional surgery, I was longing to meet my daughter. When I mentioned that to my ICU nurse, she was incredulous. She immediately made arrangements to take me up to see her and touch her for the first time and even insisted on taking pictures for me. Her act of kindness is something I will never forget.

While I stabilized within twenty-four hours, my daughter spent ten days in NICU as her lungs built up the strength to breathe on their own. The day we brought her home was one of the best days of my life. Finally, our little family was all together.

Then, it was time to get back to work. Opposing counsel still needed responses, and clients still expected me to have their interests at the top of my priority list. Four weeks after giving birth, I started working two days a week. I knew that if I waited too long, there wouldn't be any business to come back to.

During this time, well-meaning colleagues, most of them men my mother's age, encouraged me to close shop or merge with another firm. They thought I needed security. No one would blame me for deciding this was all too much for me to do as a solo practitioner. But I saw it as a slap in the face and an insult to my mother's legacy. She had worked so hard for so long and was so proud of the firm she kept running for almost twenty years. I couldn't give up now.

I was learning what it was like to be a motherless daughter, a mother to a daughter, and a business owner all at once. Three new hats, all of them life-changing events in their own right. There are some days when I wonder if I am doing any of them well.

Seven weeks after giving birth, I had my first probate hearing. I was opening a dependent administration in an estate where the husband was killed in a car accident, leaving behind a wife and three children, two of whom were minors. While wading through my own grief, I was also helping my clients navigate their own recently upturned worlds.

A few weeks after that, while encouraging my child to tolerate tummy time, an opposing counsel called my cell phone. I warned her she might be hearing some extra noises but not to be alarmed—and I made an offhand comment about how I am sure she did the same thing when her kids were born. Her flat reply was that, no, she didn't think about cases when her kids were that little, which left me feeling both jealous and resentful. She worked at a big firm, and whatever their other challenges may be, at least she didn't have to worry about single-handedly keeping a business afloat weeks after having a child.

The nice thing about owning your own business is that, to an extent, you can make your own hours and work when you can. As a mother, that type of flexibility is very important. It doesn't always work out that way—when you have depositions or are preparing for trial, you don't have a choice—but, on your average day, I wanted to be able to spend time with my kid. Many days, I will stop working a little early so that I can pick up my kid and take her to the park. Then, after she goes to bed, I finish up whatever tasks need to be done.

The reality that I was now the only attorney in the office was hitting hard. In the first seven years of practicing law, I had a smart, thirty-year trial attorney at my disposal to ask questions whenever they arose. Now, seemingly overnight, it was just me.

But it also created unique opportunities. Soon after I returned to work full-time, a new client reached out to our office. Like my mother, her mother was dying of a brain tumor, albeit a different type. Her case was strong and compelling but required some time-sensitive legal maneuvering I wasn't comfortable attempting on my own. I soon found myself co-counsel with another lawyer mom not much older than I was. Working with another attorney who wasn't my mother not only showed me different ways to approach problems but also made me feel better about my own abilities.

Most days, I am so proud of how well I've handled the many changes in my life. Overall, my business revenue is up significantly, even with all of the setbacks. Our firm has the privilege of turning away more cases than it takes—a significant milestone. I get to choose which clients and cases I work with instead of being forced to take on things that don't feel right because we need the money. Most of my clients are genuinely grateful to work with us, and our team has never felt more cohesive.

But, like many professional women, imposter syndrome looms behind me. No matter how many awards I win or how many clients tell me how grateful they are, I can't help but feel that they are only saying those things or giving me the award because they feel sorry for me. Sometimes, I feel like I will never be the lawyer I would have been if I had been able to work with Mom longer and learned more from her. She was a talented litigator who made everything look easy. Meanwhile, I find myself having to research basic issues more often than I would like.

Every milestone, both as a mother and a lawyer, is also a reminder that my own mother is no longer here. When my niece turned two, I started crying when we sang "Happy Birthday." My mother would have loved to be there, laughing and smiling with everyone else. When my mother-in-law (whom I adore) splashes with my daughter in the pool, it almost brings me to tears—Mom, an avid scuba diver, loved swimming with my nephews and getting them comfortable in the water.

Some days, it's easy to want to throw in the towel. The idea of having someone else responsible for my clients, my employees, and my paycheck is alluring. Then I'll win a hearing, receive a heartfelt note from a client, or get a call from someone who just learned of Mom's passing and wanted to reach out to tell me how proud she would be of me.

Recently, I came across something my mother wrote when she was twenty. She hoped "to become the best female trial attorney in the State of Texas, to have children and prove you can combine a career and motherhood." There is no doubt in my mind that she accomplished that goal, and every day, I am proving that it can stretch across generations.

When I look at my daughter and see my Mom's eyes staring back at me, I am reminded of how hard she fought for me and my siblings and, most importantly, how hard she fought for herself. I hope that my daughter also looks back on having a mother as a lawyer and feels both proud and grateful, and I teach her the value of resilience and determination.

Caitlin Haney Johnston

Native Austinite Caitlin Haney Johnston is a four-time *Austin Monthly* Top Attorney, Winner of the 2021 Austin Under Forty Awards in the Legal Category, and Texas Super Lawyer Rising Star in 2024. She has also been named a Pathfinder by the Travis County Women Lawyers Association. Her practice focuses on estate planning, probate, and probate litigation.

Through both personal and professional experience, she understands the importance of planning when staring down a diagnosis as well as the everyday concerns of parents with young children. She takes a practical but empathetic approach to walking families through difficult situations. She believes in providing quality legal services to all types of individuals and families. A co-founder of the Cancer Law Clinic, Caitlin gives back to the community in a variety of ways. She is a frequent speaker on estate planning and probate topics.

www.thehaneylawfirm.com

6

Feeling Beyond Pen and Paper

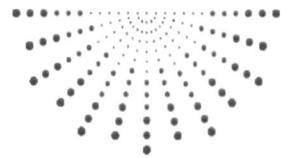

Nadia Bettac

My face burns with the anger consuming me. *Why am I the only one who needs to see a therapist?* I sit in front of my computer. My eyes close, my chest tightens, and I feel like running away. The computer screen glows, and the keyboard awaits my command. My fingers are not quite ready to type; instead, I reflect on how I got to this point. I realize that if I don't do something to change, I can't move forward. I don't want to say what I feel out loud because it would make it real, but *maybe they would be better off without me here*. I've done this search before, but never fully committed. Forcing my hand to move the mouse, I click on the search bar and type, *therapist Austin*.

Since graduating from law school in 2009 and becoming a mom, the demands of work and family have caused me to feel anger, anxiety, frustration, and depression when my expectations are not met. I have become exhausted from having the same arguments with my husband surrounding our clash of perspectives and expectations of each other. My expectations, I realize now, were never going to be attainable because I expect perfection. I am constantly trying to please people at the expense of my own happiness, but I don't know how to resolve it anymore.

My parents came from Guyana to the United States and worked very hard to provide for me and my brothers. And they expected us to work hard in return. Even though I grew up in a supportive home, open communication and discussion about mental health didn't exist. We never had calm discussions but rather heated conversations filled with anger. "I'm right! You're just wrong." Doors slammed and silent treatments permeated the house. So, as a product of my environment, I also communicated with anger and defensiveness.

As for mental health and well-being, minority families have different cultural perceptions. They often speak about adversities they faced when becoming successful. Because they faced those adversities, which are perceived as being more difficult than what the younger generation faced, they feel as if the younger generation just needs to suck it up. Mental health issues and seeking treatment are viewed as weaknesses. Any time depression would come up in our circle, I'd hear the same responses:

"Depressed? You mean you're just having a bad day? It will be better tomorrow."

"Depressed? You just need to eat."

"Depressed? Why don't you just feel happy? If you feel happy, you can be happy."

"Depressed? Antidepressants are not the answer. Exercise."

"Depressed? What do *you* have to be depressed about? You have everything you need."

Because depression was skirted, I became a master at gaslighting my own feelings. Invalidating my feelings caused me to question my emotional well-being and exacerbated my depression. Attending college and eventually law school added a new layer of stress, with the added pressure of a heavy workload and even higher expectations for myself.

As a kid, since I couldn't communicate my feelings, especially without anger, I turned to journaling. Knowing how to resolve the feelings beyond just writing about them was not something I had learned, but journaling gave me a way to process my feelings for myself. It had been a while since I kept a journal because somehow my family always found them and read them, but as an adult with adult-sized problems, I needed a place to let out the thoughts I was too afraid to say out loud.

Journal Entry

January 1, 2013

The start of a new year and I hope that this year is better for me. I bought this journal at Barnes and Noble in hopes that by writing my thoughts that I may feel better and when I look back at this a year from now I won't be so sad. There are things that bother me and I worry. I have realized that I am truly alone. No one to hang out with. Even if I moved it would be the same. People seemed to have forgotten about me. There is [boyfriend] but that relationship is so messed up. It makes me so, so, so sad. He was supposed to be the one. I miss him as my boyfriend. I hate being alone. Work sucks. I don't think I was made to be a lawyer. I am having serious doubts. I constantly feel stupid. I guess I should be happy that I have a job. I am depressed...I cry a lot. Please let 2013 be better.

The blue ink stood bold on the stark white page. Reading it now, even though I wrote the word, I struggled to admit it: *depressed*. The truth is, I never wanted to be a personal injury lawyer. I thought I would be a corporate lawyer doing corporate things. Spoiler alert: if you go to a fourth-tier law school, no one from big law wants to hire you out of law school, even if you passed your state's bar exam. Even if you passed two state bar exams. It was almost four years since graduating from law school, and I was stuck doing a job I did not like. And my relationship? Toxic. I was still holding onto that relationship in hopes that it would be a fairy tale ending, all while my gut was saying, "Stupid, he is cheating on you...again." I was caught in a vicious cycle. So, I just kept writing and never really told anyone how I felt.

Journal Entry

February 4, 2013

It is now the first week in February. The first week before my first trial as first chair and I want to throw up. I constantly feel like I'm going to get outsmarted or tricked. I hope and pray for the best. Ugh. Why did I decide to become a lawyer...

Imposter syndrome consumed me. It still does. Navigating the litigation landscape as a minority female proved challenging, especially when my mentors were male attorneys, and it was rare in personal injury to have female lawyers as colleagues or opposing counsel. It's hard to feel confident when you don't have anyone like you to model your trial style and skills.

The February trial was a successful verdict for my client, and I was offered a job. The change of employer allowed for a more supportive environment that I didn't have before. When I would go to trial and win, it was celebrated. I felt rewarded even though the trials gave me anxiety and made me physically sick. Overall, things started feeling better.

Journal Entry

May 27, 2013

I don't really know what or how to write. To have the realization that I have anxiety and am truly depressed is one thing, but not having the ability or knowledge on how to solve the problem is truly the issue. I feel like I should be moving forward. Some parts of me are, but some parts of me are not. I want to move forward with finding a husband and having a personal life and not just working. However, parts of me feel like this will never happen. Maybe it's me and my issue. I don't know how to solve it. I need to prepare myself for this uncertain future, but I don't know how long I can live like this or live this life. I am not meant for this life or this profession. Everything bothers me. I have a lack of motivation and will.

It's so clear now that even a change of jobs and ending my toxic relationship were not going to solve my problems. I wanted more, and I felt like everyone else wanted more for me, too. Culturally, people in my family got married and started a family at a young age due to financial circumstances, and because of this, education took a backseat. For example, my mom was seventeen when she married my dad. My great-aunt was married at fourteen and had all five of her kids by age twenty-two. However, when my parents came to the United States, education was first for their children, even when there was pressure about marriage.

Law school was over, and I had a job. Naturally, it was time to be married and have kids, but I was so far from this expectation.

Journal Entry

January 4, 2014

It amazes me as I sit here and write that nothing really has changed since the last I wrote. I have made promises and goals that 2014 would be different. We will see. I am tired of tears, sadness, and loneliness. I feel like things will never get better. I hope they will change. Please.

This was the last entry I made in my journal. It was my breaking point from writing in my journal, but not enough to seek outside help. I decided to make changes because I didn't want to feel this way anymore. The only place I admitted to feeling depressed was in this journal, and if I didn't write about it, maybe it would cease to exist. The promises and goals that I made were to focus on myself, make new friends, and just accept litigation as part of my life. I set out to find a husband by joining young professional groups and volunteering. If the person was volunteering, likely they were a good person.

I continued to litigate cases successfully. I was a workhorse, and litigation required it. Long hours, late nights, and early mornings were all the norm. Since I didn't have any other obligations, I was there for it all. It was not an uncommon occurrence that after trial, the opposing counsel wanted to hire me and jurors asked for my card. I would smile and politely respond that I could not, but it did feel amazing. I dedicated myself to volunteering in legal groups and taking on leadership positions. At the University of Texas School of Law, I became a mock trial coach and eventually an adjunct professor. If I was going to stay in this profession, I had to give it all.

One of the service groups finally paid off in my search for a husband. At a fundraiser, my husband, invited by a mutual friend, showed up without knowing it was a fundraiser and cash to pay the cover. Later we found ourselves at a casino table, and when I egged on our mutual friend to bet by exclaiming, "Bet, you little bitch," I piqued my husband's interest. The magic of Facebook Messenger allowed us to meet a few days later, and within a year and a month, we were married. Finally, the life I wanted and craved was coming to fruition.

After spending over a year as just the two of us, traveling and enjoying the excitement of being newly married, my husband and I were ready to start a family. I never placed much thought on motherhood or how I would be as a mom. Since I came from a family where the women had multiple children and also worked, I was confident I could be successful as well. When I did not get pregnant right away, I put a lot of pressure on myself and created ovulation charts and bought every kind of ovulation test and pregnancy test. After a night of celebrating my husband's birthday and a fair amount of wine, I found out I was pregnant.

Prior to my pregnancy, it never occurred to me how unsupportive the litigation environment was for expecting and working mothers. I found myself trying to balance the long hours and unpredictable schedule while battling the physical changes my body was going through, including the urge to take a nap. Childcare and flexible work arrangements were limited. The workplace and courthouse didn't have mom rooms or pump spaces. Opposing counsels struggled with the idea of maternity leave because the cases would either be delayed or covered by someone else.

I realized that the cases and demands in litigation would not lighten up, so I switched to working in subrogation. I wanted some sense of calm with my baby, and subrogation would be it. It was formulaic—no battles to be fought or won—I just had to keep my head down and try to recoup some money, then leave at the end of the day when I said I would.

When my son was born, my emotions were mixed between excitement and fear. My expectation for myself was to be the best mother I could be, but my mind would shift focus to where I felt I was falling short.

One night, shortly after returning home from the hospital, I stole away to take a shower while my new baby slept. The water felt so warm across my skin. The water in the shower at the hospital was so lukewarm, but the water in my own shower was a refreshing spa compared to that cold hospital room. I poured the shampoo and started to run my hands through my hair. Then, I heard it. It was a sound so loud that I couldn't figure out what was going on. Then my brain slowly pieced it together. Crying. I instantly turned off the water, worried about my baby. But the crying stopped. What is happening? I stood there alone, confused. Okay, I should go check on him. I got my towel, jumped out of the shower, and padded down the hallway. Still, I heard silence.

"Is he okay?" I shouted.

"He's fine," my husband responded.

He's fine. I questioned what had just happened as I walked back to my shower. My hand reached for the knob, turning it slowly. The water began again. And so did the crying noise. My eyes raised, but at this point, I was cold. Just wanting a hot shower and a little unsure of what was happening, I hopped back in and felt warmth on my face, but not from the water. I had begun to cry.

How could I be a good mom if I didn't even know when my baby was crying? Should I bring him in here so that I can see him? What if he is hungry? I don't really know what he needs. I don't know my own baby.

During maternity leave, I found myself thinking about work when I would get a moment to myself. Although human resources had warned me not to look at my email, I was worried and stressed about getting behind, so I would respond here and there. *I could still get a little bit done and be viewed as successful for my review.* Maternity leave ended as everyone else was on holiday leave. The short-term leave email was very clear that I must physically return to the office when my maternity leave ended or else my job would be terminated. So here I was in an empty office, and I missed my baby. The dinging noise went off on my cell phone. It was time. I pulled the supplies from my brand new Sarah Wells bag that stored my pump and began my routine. The supply was slim, which left me disappointed and feeling like I let my baby down.

For a year, I stuck with the boring but predictable, but it allowed me to be a mom. Though, at every turn, I doubted myself as to whether or not I was making the best decisions—food, daycare, reading time, routines, experiences for him to learn and grow, etc. As my doubts grew, I worried that I had left my baby permanently scarred. Eventually, at work, the boring but predictable became not a great fit, but I didn't know what else to do.

"Go back to school. Get an MBA," said my husband.

"That's the last thing I need. I am not good at school. I have never been. I am not good at tests either," I responded.

"You just keep making excuses. You can do it."

"I do not want to do it. I know myself. Plus, the GMAT requires math. I am not good at math."

There was the cycle—trying to give one hundred percent to being a good mom and one hundred percent to being the lawyer version of me that I had worked hard to achieve. However, I didn't know who I was right now. What I did know was that I did not like my career choice, and the first year of parenting was incredibly difficult. Balancing both being successful at raising a child and being successful at work often clashed. And I realized that I couldn't give both being a mom and my career one hundred percent. I was failing at both.

"You are depressed. You should talk to someone," my husband would tell me.

"You just think I am crazy. I am not crazy. I don't need to see someone. I am allowed to feel how I feel."

"I don't think you are crazy, but you should talk to someone."

It went back and forth for a while until I ended up going back to what I knew because I was too tired to expend energy on something new. "Oh, hello, insurance defense litigation. I've missed you, old friend." Of course, I didn't really miss it, but it was the only area of law I knew how to do well.

The next few years of litigation were less than stellar. The good days were manageable, and the bad days were completely rough. By day, I was a lawyer, and at night, I turned on a switch and had to be a mom and wife, and sometimes back to being a lawyer when there were late-night work duties. There were days when I was just too tired to do it. There were days when the two spilled over one another and competed for my attention. Because of this, I lacked patience and would just lash out with frustration and anger instead.

As our roles as parents were ever-changing, so was our routine, but we needed a strong one to make our day-to-day responsibilities work. After bedtime, I would continue working on my cases, answering emails, and preparing for the next day. With the number of cases, I could never catch up. That did not stop me from trying. *This was my job as a lawyer.* My job required a lot of driving, and I found myself panicking and rushing to make it home. I needed to make sure my son ate healthy, had a fun shower time, had bedtime stories because his little brain needed it, and knew he was loved. *This was my job as a mom.*

Three years into this journey of lawyering and motherhood, we, of course, entered into the coronavirus pandemic, which really blurred the lines between work and family obligations. The start of the pandemic added new stressors, which were equally shared and felt by everyone in the world.

Once, during the pandemic, I was conducting a Zoom deposition of the treating provider for a plaintiff. I tried with all of my might to schedule everything just perfectly: I would put my son down for a nap during the deposition, which would allow me to not be interrupted. He would get his rest, and I would be able to do my deposition.

The deposition started, and I was getting all of the information I needed to be effective at trial in case we didn't settle. Then it happened. It all went so fast; the door opened, and my mind knew it was him. Tiny footsteps ran quickly across the floor. Before I could say, "Can we go off the record?" my right cheek was planted with a kiss followed by a sweet "I love you, Momma." I smiled, we went off the record, and I panicked. *What do I do with this child? I need to finish this deposition!* I quickly felt angry. Angry that I was in this situation, and angry for not knowing how I was supposed to handle this all. I managed to get my husband, who was also working, to take over so I could finish the deposition, albeit quicker than I wanted, and my mind was still so focused on how the deposition was screwed up. It was this moment and others like it that finally led to the singular moment I decided to ask for help.

My computer is still glowing, waiting for me to do something. I reflect on the argument with my husband. My feelings are playing out front and center in my daily life instead of on pen and paper, like in my journals, or in my head when I stopped writing. Our exchange has happened many times.

"I am not saying you are a bad person."

"But, you don't understand. I am allowed to feel angry."

"But you are angry and depressed all the time. It makes it hard to be around you. I love you."

When my husband tells me I'm angry or depressed, I view it as a character flaw, and I don't hear anything else after that. Remember, I wasn't raised to believe in that stuff because you're supposed to work through the adversities. Things would just be fine if my husband and family could see past my emotions and listen to what I am saying. I am focusing on them and trying to make everyone happy.

My body feels defeated. My anger subsides, and sadness sinks in. *I know my husband cares, and that is why he insists I get help. I know I need to make a change and accept that these feelings are real and have consequences, or I will lose everything.* In order to make things better, I have to fix myself. It is like they say on an airplane: put on your oxygen mask first because if you don't take care of yourself first, it's harder to take care of those around you.

I launch the search, but it's all overwhelming with all of the options. *How do I know these people will help me? How do I pick the right person? What do I even write? Should I be honest? Okay, I just need to start somewhere.* I begin by filling out a few contact forms and emailing different places.

October 8, 2020

Good afternoon Ms. [therapist],

I am looking to start therapy for a variety of issues, which include anxiety, depression, anger, family (parents/siblings) and spouse, and general work issues. Are you accepting new patients? If so, I am open to doing virtual appointments and wondering how to get started. I have never done therapy before, so any help with the process would be great. Thank you and hope you are doing well.

Nadia

Well, it feels a little cathartic saying I need help and what the issues are. Apparently, I have a lot of them.

It took a few tries, but I was able to land a therapist with sessions over Zoom. Therapy surprised me because I could be real with my feelings because the sessions were confidential, sides were not chosen, and my feelings were not dismissed. There was a lot of analysis on why. *Why did I feel like I had no voice? Why did I feel like I was not good enough? Why did I have a need to give one hundred percent to everything all the time?*

Common themes started to emerge. For me, it was important to my personal fulfillment to have my voice heard in both my professional and personal life. It was also important to me to be successful at both. I was wanting perfection. Feeling like I was not enough and the perception of failing contributed to my depression. Since I never addressed it, I let it explode.

Therapy provided new tools that allowed me to see things in a different way and then problem-solve without resorting to anger and defensiveness. Advocating for my feelings and communicating them allowed me not to go down the path of anger and depression. For example, we would role-play a situation, and I would explain what I anticipated the reaction to be, but then I was asked to take on the role of the person reacting and focus on their why. Focusing on the why required me to adjust how I reacted to the information being told to me. Communicating my feelings back guided how the other person responded back to me. It was kind of like law school all over again, rewiring how you think and approach a problem. Recognizing the importance of effective communication has allowed me to tailor my conversations with my husband, my son, and my family. As part of advocating for my feelings, I had to recognize what triggered them in the first place. When recognizing the triggers, instead of anger, I could audibly say, "I need a moment," take a break, and come back to parenting or discussions with my husband.

Setting up and maintaining boundaries was also something important I needed to do at work and home. I'm a people pleaser because I mainly wanted to avoid conflict and felt pressure that people expected me to be a certain way. It was revealed to me, however, that I couldn't give one hundred percent to all of the important things in my life all the time at the same time. As an example, when it came to my work calendar I people-pleased because it was a litigation expectation. "Do you want all of the parties' depositions on the same day?" "Sure!" Not anymore. I reduced the number of depositions a day and required a start time after my son's school would start, and the depositions needed to be completed before the end of the day. When I implemented this, people whined, but I held firm, and this didn't change the outcome of the case.

Continuing on the path of setting boundaries, I reduced after-work activities and took a step back on leadership roles. I became comfortable with setting family boundaries as well by saying no to things I didn't want to do, like attending every family event. Shifting my focus away from pleasing people by prioritizing my own well-being allowed me to relax, which in turn reduced my stress.

We addressed my feelings of inadequacy in raising my son. The discussion shifted to what my husband and I were providing—experiences and memories—those milestones should be celebrated. Because I worked, I had to accept that it was okay that he used an iPad. It was okay for him to not have a home-cooked meal. At the end of the day, as long as I was there for him, that's what mattered.

There is no shame in asking for help, seeking therapy, or letting others know how you feel. Having the confidence to say that my feelings are tied to anxiety and depression helped me have the discussion more openly with my family. They, in turn, became more receptive to the idea and explored their own solutions when dealing with their own feelings. It felt great to redirect the narrative around mental health.

Juggling the demands of a demanding profession with the responsibilities of marriage and parenting will always require physical and mental energy, but therapy became a valuable tool to manage the stressors, manage my expectations, and manage my goals. As my marriage, my role as a mother, and my job in the legal profession continually change and present new challenges, therapy gave me the confidence to tackle these issues beyond writing my emotions down on paper.

Nadia Bettac

Nadia Bettac is a highly accomplished personal injury litigator and adjunct professor at the University of Texas School of Law. She owns her own law firm and mediation practice, Bettac Advocacy and Mediation, PLLC.

Volunteering in her community and advocating for diversity has been her passion since childhood. She is an award-winning director for the Austin Young Lawyers Association and continues her passion through various projects with the Austin Young Lawyers Association and the Austin Bar Association.

Nadia enjoys spending time with her husband and son, who keep her adventurous.

https://www.facebook.com/nadiaramkissoon

https://www.facebook.com/profile.php?id=100093284655621

https://www.linkedin.com/in/nadiabettac/

https://www.linkedin.com/company/bettac-advocacy-and-mediation-pllc/

https://www.instagram.com/nadia_bettac/

https://twitter.com/NadiaRamkissoon

7

Live Like That

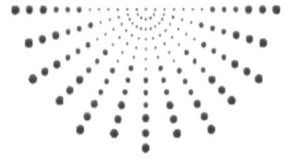

Laura Ramos James

"How can you live like that?"

A convergence of feelings stirs inside me upon hearing this question. My husband Jon asks me this after we've put our kids to bed. The night couldn't be any darker or the house any quieter. I had already magically erased the aftermath of dinner with a toddler and a self-feeding baby as if it had never been there. Jon and I are sitting in our living room as I anxiously wait to enjoy some mindless TV. The momentum gained from the combination of coffee and adrenaline throughout the day has long worn off, as has my makeup.

Immediately upon hearing the question, I take a slow inhale, filling up my lungs halfway with air, raising my chin, beaming a little, and I get the faintest desire to smile for a fleeting minute. The initial feeling that takes over, if ever so discreetly, is...pride?

Frankly, it really is hard for most people to balance even half of what I have on my plate. Much less to do it so seemingly successfully, so smoothly. "*She makes it look easy*" is how friends and work acquaintances describe their perception of my ability to run a household, raise two small and happy children, and build and run a law firm while still practicing as a trial lawyer.

And then, like a bolt from out of the blue, the sweet, sweet feeling of pride turns to sour and uncomfortable shame. I realize Jon is not asking this question as an implied compliment. He's concerned for his wife, the mother of his children, who seems to be running on fumes. If I'm honest, both of us are concerned.

I think back on how the day went. Flashbacks of a handful of moments come to me, one by one but in rapid succession, like machine gun shots: pow...replying to a work email on my phone, pow...while packing a lunch box, pow...asking my husband not to talk to me because I am busy and pow...rushing my toddler to hurry up because we're late. A beautiful sunny and crisp Texas December morning with my beautiful family is completely lost on me, consumed by the stress and pressure of whether we will be able to get out of the park before everyone's hungry and whining. Pow...unable to let go of the half-written motion I couldn't finish because the girls woke up too early. Nobody is having fun right now, not even me. When did I become so uptight? How did I get here? Who *can* live like this? Is it worth it?

1989 – The origin of "living like this"

When I was a little girl, one of my favorite games was playing "secretary," a game I played with my best friend and neighbor, Lucia, who was a couple of years older than I was. A bed would serve as our pretend desk, and on top of it, we'd lay used-up notepads that we found around our houses. Lucia's family had some involvement with a printing business, so extra paper was always easy to come by, and we *loved* paper. We'd get pens, too, of course. Phones that no longer worked and were stored in the garage as well as TV antennas, old walkie-talkies, old intercom systems—any item that looked tech-related because we were trying to run a state-of-the-art office. How would a secretary "run" an office, you ask? Well, we did. In our world, one with no female role model who was the "boss," the "CEO," or the "partner," the only thing we knew was that secretaries worked in an office setting, which is what we wanted, but these secretaries were actually going to be playing boss.

Looking back now, I know that my dad is responsible for my wild, unfettered belief that I could and would do anything I wanted in life, even if it was something I had never seen done before. I remember feeling immense sadness for the many dogs that roamed the streets of my hometown. When I asked my dad why the President wasn't doing something about it, he told me when *I* was president, *I* could do something about it. He didn't laugh or give any indication this statement was not one hundred percent serious. I internalized the belief that if I wanted to be President, it was possible. And if that was possible, anything I wanted to achieve was, too.

Our other favorite game was "going out to sell." Sell what? We would sell stickers or notepads. We knocked on our neighbors' doors, those neighbors we didn't really know much about but who we knew were adults with money, and we sold them stickers, ones we already had. Lucia was six-and-a-half, and I was five. Times were different back then. I don't think I'll be letting my child walk around the neighborhood alone when she's five, but I grew up in a small town in Mexico called Monclova, where people didn't lock their doors and didn't think twice about letting small children roam the street or go to the corner store on their bikes.

"*Please don't do that, Laury. Our neighbors are going to think we need money or that we don't give you what you need,*" said my mom, worried about what people would think more than whether someone could abduct her child one afternoon when she was not around.

We still did it. It was exciting. It wasn't just that we felt like grownups, although that's part of it. We were driven by the transaction and the interactions. We also would offer to wash the neighbors' cars. I'm sure after we were done, their cars were dirtier than before; the perpetual flour-like dust that covers Monclova thickened and turned into a muddy consistency.

As evidenced by my childhood make-believe, I always had an entrepreneurial spirit. But that wasn't all: since I was about three years old, my parents predicted that I'd grow up to be a lawyer.

"You love to argue. Do you have to argue about everything?" My dad would say between chuckles. He and my mom still tell stories about me as a little girl wanting to pack a suitcase when we traveled. When my parents would refuse to let me take a mountain of toys and knick-knacks, I would assuredly declare that children have rights and that parents cannot stomp all over them. It seems I was destined to be a lawyer from the beginning.

Every time I saw a lawyer on TV, passionately defending his client, standing up for what was just while their client sat next to them, intimidated but proud to have someone in their corner, it inspired me. Those visuals resonated with my idea of professional fulfillment: Standing up for what is fair, righting someone's wrong.

A catastrophic dog attack that happened to me when I was three cannot be discounted as part of what ignited the fire in me to help others experiencing injustice. I had been playing in the backyard of some acquaintances of my parents who had a German Shepherd. The owners, who were at fault for the attack but wouldn't accept responsibility, shamelessly pointed fingers at my parents (who were their friends) and at the dog's own nature. I was just old enough when the attack happened to remember it vividly. I always knew, and certainly know now, that my parents were not at fault. I know the dog was not at fault. But I know irresponsible pet owners when I see them now. And through the disfiguring injuries I sustained, I know physical pain, too. The name-calling and looks of pity I got because of the bandages and stitches on my face exposed me to emotional pain and gave me scars that ran much deeper than the physical ones.

Helping an injured victim get justice through the legal system against the people or companies who wronged them is a way that I can fight for those who can't fight for themselves. I've always had a passion for fighting for those who are seeking justice.

Looking back to my childhood, it is clear as day now that I'd become a mom if given the opportunity. Even though the idea of having children wasn't something I thought I'd do when I was growing up, I always treated our family dogs like they were my babies. I never really played with dolls when I was little, but I loved our dogs, babying them and even being overly protective of them. I see that was the natural mothering instinct in me, although I didn't see it at the time. I know I was meant to be a mother, and it has ultimately become the most important role of my life.

There's no question that my childhood dreams of enterprise, law, and motherhood came true. But it took a lot of tears, frustration, despair, resilience, determination, heartbreak, sacrifice, and loss. And no rainbows or unicorns appeared when they finally came true. My dreams, in real life, look quite different from those I envisioned when I was a young girl, going door to door selling stickers and learning to stand up against injustice.

2018 - Living "Like This"

Sean takes a sip of his coffee after listening to me talk for twenty minutes straight. The small coffee shop is crowded on a Tuesday morning. People are either immersed in their laptops or having lively conversations. Sean probably had his reply ready nineteen minutes ago when I started talking, but he kindly let me, a bright-eyed and bushy-tailed young woman, share my dreams before imparting the wisdom he'd acquired after practicing for over two decades.

"The first thing you must decide is whether you want to be a solo practitioner or whether you want to run a law firm. Big or small, a law firm is different from being a solo. There are different challenges, and different pros and cons. They're two different animals. You need to know the answer to that to decide what route to follow," he shared with me. I pondered over this advice for the days and weeks to follow before concluding that I didn't know the answer. But I did know that after being patronized and having my opinions and experience discounted for years, I yearned for independence and professional discretion. I longed to make the decisions—everything from picking the colors of my law firm's logo, to deciding which clients I wanted to help, to whether to file a response to a motion and when to do so.

To fly solo was my initial choice. By practicing alone, I enjoyed the freedom to make decisions without having to consult anyone or even interact with anyone for hours on end if I didn't want to. As a *closeted* introvert, that is often my preference. So, I began spreading the word that I had started my own personal injury law firm, Ramos James Law, PLLC, and I was ready to help anyone with their injury cases at any time.

Soon, it became apparent that although I could remain the only lawyer, I needed a staff—a good problem to have because it meant people trusted me with their cases, and I could no longer handle both the clerical and legal work alone. So, I added paralegals and legal assistants to my team, and things were great. Until they weren't.

Often, I would meet up with colleagues for coffee or lunch to discuss our practices, personal challenges, successes, and the like. But when I felt compelled to go down the hall to talk through a specific case, or client, there was no one. There was no lawyer next to my office with whom I could talk about how a certain client's disability could be permanent, how to best present it during a deposition, how to connect her with the best specialist, and how to help her afford her surgery. It started to feel lonely.

It wasn't until I could no longer deny that I had more cases than I could handle that I knew it was time to make a shift. I either needed to hire a contract attorney to help me as a solo practitioner or change my mind and become a "two or more attorney" law firm.

...and this is when I made the decision that Sean wisely shared with me that busy Tuesday morning at the coffee shop. And I've never looked back.

Enter the scene: my first associate, "George." George was wonderful: hard-working, kind, and eager to help injury victims from disadvantaged communities. Like a well-watered plant, the law firm was growing. We had enough cases for three lawyers and then some, but George and I worked compulsively and were able to handle our docket with just the two of us and our support staff. We had each other's back and relished what we were doing together for our clients.

Right when we felt we were bursting at the seams, unable to take on any more clients, a blood test confirmed the most exciting news of my life: I was pregnant.

I was thrilled and nervous about the prospect of my life changing forever with the addition of a whole new human to my and my husband's lives. The magnificence of a healthy pregnancy allowed me to continue to work at the same pace I'd been at for the past decade, at 100 mph.

When I was a little over six months pregnant, I started to prepare in case I had to be "out of commission" for a few days due to any potential complications with childbirth. I had worked almost nonstop since high school, and the thought of not working for more than a few days simply did not exist. As an example, a potential new client called me while I was in the middle of my bachelorette trip, and instead of declining the call or asking the client to call back at another time, I went to a separate room to handle the call and opened the new case right there on my laptop. Not yet a mom, I had no understanding or expectation of what it would even entail. Being on call around the clock for anything other than the law firm, a non-human dependent, was a concept that had not yet registered in my mind. I knew that I would need to step away from work, although I wasn't sure how it would look. Surely, I'd had my generous share of late nights in college and law school. But I didn't have a clue about the grueling sleep deprivation that comes with being a new parent. When more seasoned parents talk to parents-to-be, they usually make remarks like: "Enjoy your sleep now!" Those remarks are inadequate to prepare you for what's to come, which is life as a zombie.

As I was making what I naively considered appropriate arrangements for the birth of a child, and putting some thought into a temporary "Out of Office" automated email reply, my associate called me to drop a bomb in my lap. He was quitting to join his law school buddy at a competitor's firm in just a few days. You could've knocked me down with a feather. The feeling was much like what I imagine it would feel like to be woken up from a deep sleep by a bucket of iced water thrown on you. His decision came during the middle of the pandemic, so I was already in fight or flight mode daily. A large percentage of our business consisted of helping people who were hurt during a car crash, yet during the pandemic, driving was down ninety-eight percent. The uncertainty of whether our business model would survive was part of our every move. Adding to the equation that now I would have minus one lawyer certainly didn't help.

Losing my only associate was already difficult, but losing a paralegal to law school and another who demanded an increase of three times the benefits and pay made work even more stressful. We struggled trying to get out of a commercial lease for a building we were only using at five percent capacity during Covid. On top of all of it, the stress was compounded by having to implement new systems and protocols for everything from accepting law firm calls from our homes, to having clients who were not tech-savvy sign contracts electronically, to managing bank deposits when our bank had nothing but a skeleton crew. The challenges were endless, like a game of whack-a-mole, but instead of tokens, my law license, livelihood, and sanity were at stake.

Having a healthy pregnancy through it all was a blessing, and I only understood how much of a blessing it was after my second pregnancy wasn't as healthy years later. Still, the insomnia and raging hormones that came with the pregnancy did not make it a walk in the park. I held it together as best I could, trying to do all the things.

But when my dad called and told me he didn't think my mom would make it after she'd fallen into a coma only a few weeks before my first baby was born, that was when the Jenga tower came crashing down inside me. Whatever I had been able to hold together toppled over, not piece by piece or in slow motion, but all at once.

I was lying down in bed with a few pillows behind me and my laptop perched on top of my huge belly, the only position I could work from for longer than thirty minutes without having to move around too much. When I hung up the phone, Jon heard me wail in distress and ran into the room.

"I am so sorry, honey," he said as he rushed to hug me. I remember looking up, explaining what I'd been told, and seeing him tear up, showing genuine sadness and empathy. I felt held and loved and supported. I felt like I could stop and grieve to my heart's desire, lament, cry, scream, relive every memory over and over, and that someone would take care of everything else. Except that I couldn't.

My OBGYN, who knew the anguish I was experiencing about my mom being so ill, had admonished me to do everything I could to stay calm and not scream or cry hard because that would be risky for me and the baby. But there were some moments when I just hurt so badly, so profoundly, that I wanted to fall asleep and never wake up. I could not bring myself to stop crying, much less to smile for my baby, who was due soon. The moments we waited in uncertainty were some of the hardest days of my life. Ultimately, my mother came out of her coma shortly after my baby was born. She made a marvelous recovery, and as Covid travel restrictions eased, she was able to come visit us and meet her first grandbaby. I'm thankful every day for the time she has with my children and with me.

To deal with hardship and stress in work and family life, some law moms turn to yoga, working out, or therapy. Some turn to their family or girlfriends, self-care, or a combination of it all. After years of learning from other law moms and from my own experience, I have concluded that there is no magic pill or hidden book of secrets on how to do it all and do it successfully. There is not even one on how to survive. You must find your own recipe for balance and stress relief, fine-tuning through trial and error, to be able to withstand the weight of your own spectacular dreams. For me, that looked like taking a deep metaphorical breath and diving into motherhood and solo law firm ownership head-on. Some days are unbelievably perfect, while a few others are perfectly horrible. But we, law moms, are not special or unique. What I mean is that steep climbs to reach goals exist in other people's lives, too, especially among those who want it all, as I do. So, back to the original dilemma: How can you live like that?

After giving birth to my first child, Victoria, the thought of becoming a stay-at-home mom crossed my mind. And like a shooting star, it was fleeting and never to be seen again after a few days of being back at work.

I find deep personal fulfillment from my work. The drive to help others who have been injured and are seeking justice gives me a purpose in life. For instance, I once handed over a settlement check to a man who, with tears in his eyes, told me he finally felt like a man again, like someone who could support his family and lift the weight off his wife's shoulders. This man had to let go of being the breadwinner after a wreck destroyed his means of transportation and impaired his ability to make a living doing the only thing he knew how to do, manual labor. A man whom I came to know well after handling his case for several years and spending hours upon hours together preparing for depositions, mediation, and a likely trial, and who was always stoic in his demeanor and interactions. His feeling of overwhelming joy when the settlement came thanks to my hard work and dedication is invaluable. Every time we successfully close a case for an injury victim, I'm overwhelmed by the feeling that every sacrifice has been worth it. I choose to be there for my clients.

"Thank you for the food that you made me, Mommy. I love you," beams my three-year-old at dinner as she hangs from my neck and kisses my cheek. I choose to cook this evening, and she's old enough now to tell this is not McDonald's and Mommy actually made this for her (full disclosure—it's just spaghetti and meat sauce, but I will take the credit for this "home-cooked" *meal*). The sweetest and most innocent little voice. How could I not try to cook every chance I could just to recreate this moment of gratitude, the feeling that I matter, that I am seen by her? I consciously chose to be there for my daughter when my phone is going off, dinging incessantly with work emails, texts, and calls. I chose to cook tonight as I can barely catch my breath between straightening up the house and preparing an argument to respond to a motion in my head while I pace between every room in the house. I crack my neck and rub it as I pace. Bad posture and stress have taken their toll throughout the years. But I choose to be there for my family.

And to be honest, the second Victoria thanks me for dinner, my entire body relaxes, no deadline is worth it at this moment. It's thanks to moments like this that everything else seems so small, every loss justifiable, and every moment of despair tolerable.

Tonight, I don't have an answer for Jon's question: "How can you live like that?" Yes, my life is full: full of love and purpose but also stress and chaos. And I'm not opposed to trying one, some, or all the perfectly reasonable solutions or "fine-tuning" that exist to better a law mom's life. I just can't see myself giving up any of these things that I've dreamed about my whole life, the things that make me whole and bring me joy. So, for now, all I do is get a makeup remover towelette and take off what remains of my makeup. Tomorrow will be a new day to live like this.

Laura Ramos James

Laura Ramos James is the founder and owner of Ramos James Law, PLLC, an award-winning personal injury law firm headquartered in Austin, Texas. Laura's law firm handles serious injury and death cases, recovering millions of dollars for their clients each year.

Laura has been named Up-and-Coming 100: Texas Rising Stars: 2023 & 2024 and Up-and-Coming 50: Women Texas Rising Stars: 2023 &2024 by Super Lawyers™ and been recognized as "Top Personal Injury Attorney", "Woman Leader of the Year", and "Changemaker" by different organizations. As a survivor of a catastrophic injury, Laura can uniquely relate to her clients and help them navigate their injury cases. For Laura, the most significant and transforming influence in her life has been becoming the mother of two little girls with her husband Jon. Laura is a frequent speaker and guest at lawyer and non-profit organizations as well as various podcasts.

https://www.instagram.com/law_law_land_tx/?hl=en

https://www.facebook.com/severeinjurylawyer/

https://www.linkedin.com/in/laura-ramos-james-b1807012a

https://www.ramosjames.com/

8
The Final Straw

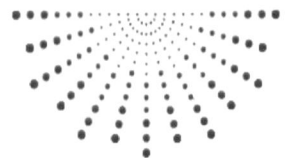

Sarah Soucie Eyberg

So this is what they mean by rock bottom, I thought as I lay next to my sleeping daughter in her bed. My cheeks burned with shame, and tears flowed down my temples into my hair. I sought solace in her room because, even though I felt like the world's shittiest human being, I knew I was still a good mother—especially in her eyes.

I couldn't bear to face my husband, who earlier that evening found me passed out in our family van in the parking lot of a brewery/event space—dead cell phone and barely coherent. He had tracked my last known location and asked for a ride from one of my best friends so he'd be able to get our vehicle home.

My initial reaction? I was pissed.

He humiliated me. Not only had he inconvenienced this friend—this VERY PREGNANT friend—but also a second good friend of mine to sit at home with our sleeping children while he went on this excursion twenty miles into the city. My friends had a front-row seat to my sloppy drunk ass and dysfunctional marriage.

But I deserved to let a little loose. I mean, geez. I work really hard. And I am the primary caregiver for our kids. I am always there for my family. I had been out all day at a professional leadership development event for new lawyers, which I helped plan and execute. Why shouldn't I carouse a little? And I wasn't the only one doing so. I was out with four others who had helped with the event, and we were all having a good, but still professional, time out.

But as the hours wore on, and as I continually told my husband I would be wrapping up soon or would only stay a little longer, he became more and more concerned.

I insisted I was doing fine and would be home soon, but could he do bedtime without me? "Sarah, if you love our kids, please just don't drive."

How silly. I am an adult. I wasn't doing street drugs or drinking during the day or keeping bottles of booze in my desk. I have never missed an important deadline or hearing or client meeting. I don't have a "problem."

Eventually, I stopped answering altogether. Not a conscious choice; I just lost track. I was having a great time!

Meanwhile, Jason could see where I was (thank goodness for Apple Find My Friends) but it wasn't like me to not answer. He reached out to my father to see if he was able to get ahold of me, and when that didn't work either, he decided to take action.

Fortunately, we are blessed with good friends, and even though it was after the kids' bedtime, Colleen came to sit at the house with our sleeping children, and Amber drove him to Minneapolis to find me. When they arrived on site, I was no longer inside the venue. They found me asleep in our van in the back of the parking lot.

I caught Amber's eye as I buckled myself into the passenger seat. I tried for a smile, tried to act like this was all so silly of my silly husband, just worried for nothing. And I am sure she saw right through that weak-ass shit.

And again, I was mad. I was embarrassed. He was overreacting. I am an adult. So what if my phone died? He knew where I was. So what if I stopped responding? It was a *professional event*, not a strip club. It wasn't even a girls night. It was all so unnecessary.

If I sound like a pouty brat, that was definitely the vibe.

My husband was exceedingly reasonable, given how angry he was with me. Once we were on the way home, he calmly explained his distress with how intoxicated I was becoming based on my text messages and increased uneasiness when I failed to respond at all. Then, when my phone began to ring straight to voicemail, he called in backup.

The more he talked, the smaller I felt. When I realized how concerned and scared he had been, I felt sick. I could hardly speak for the shame. I very rarely screwed up like this, but there had been some similar occasions in recent months. Several weeks prior to this, at a law fraternity event, I made an incredibly hurtful comment about some very dear friends' marriage that I would never have said sober. Years later, I am still fortunate to call them my friends, but I irretrievably damaged our closeness with that remark, and I will always regret it. Then, on Halloween of that year out with my husband, I blacked out large parts of the evening and didn't recall most of our drive home, which was scary and not in a fun spooky way. The truth is the only dysfunction in my marriage was a direct result of my drinking.

This was the final straw. I needed to take action. TONIGHT. I pulled out my phone and texted Chase, a colleague and friend who I knew was doing case management at Lawyer's Concerned for Lawyers. LCL is a Minnesota organization offering a free and confidential Lawyer Assistance Program for Minnesota lawyers, judges, law students, non-attorney legal professionals, and their immediate families with any issue causing them stress or distress in their lives. They offer not only addiction counseling services but broader mental health support and recovery services.

"I think I need to stop drinking."

He responded immediately that he was there for me and that we should connect in the morning. The hole in my chest expanded and ached, and tears flowed freely again. I knew by putting it out there, I was going to have to make good on it.

I immediately became afraid that I couldn't do it. And that is how I knew it was the right thing to do. If alcohol use was so ingrained into my daily habits and social life that I was worried about how I would function without it, that indicated a problem to me.

Problematic drinking is prevalent in the law profession. A study by The National Task Force on Law Well-Being in 2017 found "an elevated risk in the legal community for mental health and substance use disorders tightly intertwined with an alcohol-based social culture."[1] Nearly 13,000 practicing attorneys and 3,300 law students and 15 law schools were surveyed by the American Bar Association Commission on Lawyer Assistance Programs and the Hazelden Betty Ford Foundation.[2] Between twenty-one and thirty-six percent of attorney respondents qualified as "problem drinkers."[3] Twenty-eight percent of attorney respondents reported struggling with some level of depression.[4] Attorneys in the first ten years of practice reported the highest rates of problem drinking and depression.[5] What surprises me is that those numbers aren't even higher.

So, I knew I needed to do this. The question was how?

I not only had Chase's help and my husband's support, I also had my father's example to follow, again.

My dad is an attorney. I grew up watching him serve clients with his whole heart, helping injured people get recoveries that changed their lives. As a kid, I would wake up early, hours before my school day began, and he would take me with him to "beautiful G's Restaurant" in downtown Anoka, where I grew up. I would stretch out next to him on the seat of the biggest booth in the place, and he would start dictating notes and letters to his files while I slept for another hour. Then I would wake up and have oatmeal with brown sugar and raisins for breakfast, and he would drop me off at school.

Dad would also practice his portions of his opening statements for jury trials on us as kids. He would ask us whether the story he was weaving made sense. Could we understand his client? Did the story help us care about them?

He is a big reason why I became an attorney, and why I built a practice around helping some of the most vulnerable among us. He approached the practice of law as an act of service to his clients and ran his firm to serve those clients and his staff.

He showed me how to be a human before a lawyer and how to leverage my legal education to always help others.

However, the life of a trial lawyer is a stressful one, and my father was not immune.

One of the ways trial lawyers blow off steam after working hard is playing equally hard. And they did so "professionally." Growing up—and even as a law student and younger practicing attorney—I can't recall a bar association, Minnesota Trial Lawyers Association, or Inns of Court event that was not associated in some way with alcohol. There was the social hour before the event, wine and open bar during dinner, and, of course, a cocktail reception or after-party.

Some of my favorite and funniest stories about my father and his colleagues probably took place when they were all imbibing. I think there was a darkness there, too, though. An undercurrent of dysfunction that some of those colleagues might still be suffering from today.

My father learned from his father, too. I never met my Grandpa Ray, though his legend looms large in my family. Unfortunately, while Grandpa Ray had a big, bright personality, he also drank. Heavily. In time, he abandoned his family, leaving my grandmother to raise the rest of the children on her own. Grandpa Ray continued to drink and eventually took his own life.

My father wanted a different path for himself. In early 2015, he gave up drinking. He did a course of outpatient services at Hazelden Betty Ford in St. Paul. The Foundation is the nation's foremost nonprofit provider of comprehensive behavioral health care, providing support to individuals and families affected by addiction.

He also found strength and comfort in Alcoholics Anonymous. For my dad, AA provided a system and a structure to his sobriety, as well as accountability. He formed an amazing friendship with his sponsor, Lance. He also formed deep relationships with other people in the program and received fulfillment from supporting others in their sobriety.

So you can imagine his excitement when I called to tell him I was going to quit drinking. He was equal parts proud of my decision and eager to be of help. He was really looking forward to taking me to AA meetings with him. I wanted badly to make my dad proud, but I was not so enthusiastic.

My dad and I share a lot. I very much resemble the Soucie side of my family and was constantly reminded of that as a kid. We have similar personalities and ways of relating to the world. We love the outdoors and hunting. We went to the same undergraduate university, and we share a profession. We are both fiercely dedicated to our families.

However, when he invited me to AA meetings, instead of feeling comfort, I felt pressure. I always followed in Dad's footsteps and wanted something else to share. But it didn't feel right to me. There was one area that I just couldn't relate to. There was something about that word that didn't fit for me. I could not see myself in that label.

Alcoholic.

I did not dispute that I had a problem with alcohol. I could even concede being a "problem drinker," but I just could not identify with the term "alcoholic." There are very few positive associations with being an alcoholic, so maybe I was just in denial. Maybe I was just rationalizing away so I could avoid facing reality.

The last thing I wanted to do was hurt his feelings; however, I also knew my dad would want me to be honest with him. "Dad," I told him, "I really need you to give me the space right now to do this in my own way," I told him. To my immense relief, he not only agreed immediately but remained extremely supportive.

I also discussed my concerns with my LCL case manager. "I don't really feel like an alcoholic," I said. I hadn't had any cravings. I wasn't thinking about alcohol or when I would have my next drink. I wasn't missing social or work events to drink instead. What she said next turned my world on its ear. She told me that maybe I wasn't an alcoholic. "You know, you don't have to be an alcoholic to quit drinking."

Ho-ly shit. I couldn't believe it had never occurred to me before that I could quit drinking without being an alcoholic. For some reason, that unlocked a knot in my chest, and in its place, some ease entered my heart. Suddenly, the sobriety didn't have to be this dark, shameful secret I had to overcome. It could be this fulfilling, healthful thing that had the power to make a positive change in my life.

That paradigm shift had tremendous power over my sobriety journey and the story I told myself. There was suddenly a much more positive spin. I was in the driver's seat, taking control, nothing was in control of me, and that felt reassuring.

But alcohol was still enmeshed in my life, in ways I hadn't even noticed. Nearly every professional event I attended also had alcohol involved. Most of my social events with friends and family did, too. It didn't matter the season, didn't matter the reason.

I was worried about how others would perceive my sudden sobriety. I was a woman in my early thirties, so of course, the go-to reasoning would be that I was pregnant. Still carrying weight from my last pregnancy, I was especially sensitive to this.

I became an "instant mom" when I married my husband. Esme was less than a year old when we tied the knot, so I have been a part of her life since she can remember. I was the only one of my friends who had stepmother status, so I didn't have a lot of people to talk to about the transition and the difficulties of co-parenting. Growing up, my older sisters had a different father, and so I was no stranger to a blended family. And I have never had any trouble loving Esme with my whole heart. Still, it was different when I was pregnant for the first time.

Motherhood, in general, can be extremely isolating and lonely. Your body begins the journey to motherhood by housing another for months and then nourishes that other for months longer. Your body becomes permanently altered, and your identity is upended along with it. Even without the pressures of practicing law, just the pressures of mothering "correctly" may have done me in.

I often say it is the most difficult and yet fulfilling thing I have ever done. My first pregnancy was a wild one, as we discovered at just eight weeks that we were expecting twins. From there, the excitement was boundless, but so was the anxiety.

I was thirty-two weeks along when I developed spots in my vision at work one day. I lay down on the floor of an empty office in an attempt to lower my blood pressure and take some of the strain off of my body. When that didn't help, I called the OB's office, and they recommended I come in to be seen. I was admitted to the hospital later that night. Doctors were worried I was developing preeclampsia and thought my labs were borderline. Over the next six days, I used all my lawyering skills to advocate for keeping my babies cooking a little longer. When I was almost thirty-three weeks pregnant, my platelets plummeted, and I no longer had a choice. They began induction.

Roland was born at 2:17 a.m. and Mina at 2:34 a.m. the next morning, and my life was changed forever. About a year later, I was taking the testimony of a young mother who had been diagnosed with preeclampsia in her most recent pregnancy. She suffered a stroke post-birth and was still dealing with cognitive and physical deficits over two years later. *Holy shit, I could have died,* I realized, stunned.

My next pregnancy was a singleton, and much less complicated—as pregnancies go anyway. I was thirty-seven weeks pregnant at my last scheduled hearing, which took place about two and a half hours from my house. On my way home, I blew a tire and was stranded on the side of a busy highway with a full bladder as I waited for AAA to pick me up. My husband ended up meeting me and the tow truck to take me directly to a check-up appointment with our midwife group. Surprise, surprise, my blood pressure was a tad elevated, and other labs were concerning as well. Given my history, the midwives were ultra-cautious and advised admitting me to the hospital and inducing labor. It turned out that the baby wasn't ready to leave yet, though. By the next morning, my labs had stabilized, and no labor had begun, so I was released back home. Walter ended up making his debut at forty-one weeks after the midwife broke my water.

Mothering in the age of social media presents additional challenges. I was immediately inundated with information and OPINIONS about the *best* equipment, the *most nourishing* feeding technique, the *healthiest* sleep schedule, and on and on and on. And there in my hand was a device that would, at the scroll of a screen, show me endless photos, videos, blogs, and podcasts of others doing it better than me. It sometimes felt impossible not to take it personally, especially because I care so much about doing things *right*. The stakes are so high, how could I not?

And then there's the "Mommy Wine Culture" that permeates throughout social media as well. It's incredibly toxic, markedly to those already struggling. A study released in 2017 found women's "high-risk drinking," defined as four or more drinks in a single day, increased by 15.8% over a ten-year period from 2002-2012.[6] Suddenly, "Mommy's Sippy Cup" wine glass is a lot less cute.

Alcohol never prevented me from fully participating in my children's lives. I never missed sporting events or school functions. I did not drive intoxicated with them in the car. But I was less present than I could have been. Not to mention the drain on my mental acuity and emotional health. I may not have been directly harming my children with my problematic drinking, but I was less of a whole person and not my best self.

By becoming sober, I was also worried people would assume I was an alcoholic and thus less competent to do my legal work. The Minnesota Rules of Professional Responsibility (and the American Bar Association model rules) require attorneys to "provide competent representation."[7] The preamble to the ABA Model Rules sets the bar even higher. According to the ABA, "A lawyer should strive to attain the highest level of skill, to improve the law and the legal profession, and to exemplify the legal profession's ideals of public service."[8] Trying to achieve this benchmark with depression, anxiety, or a substance use disorder is like trying to win a wrestling match with one arm tied behind your back.

The fear of the perceptions of others impacting my livelihood was one of the biggest factors in why I didn't seek help or curb my drinking sooner. And I am not alone. The Hazelden Study found the two most common barriers to seeking help, as reported by respondents, were "not wanting others to find out they needed help and concerns regarding privacy or confidentiality."[9]

My one saving grace in all this is that I am a very driven, very stubborn woman. If I was going to do this, I was going to fucking do it. I tried to set myself up for success right away, and there were several key factors I put in place.

First was accountability. *Yes, I was a hot mess but don't worry because I am taking steps to fix it.* I had told Chase and LCL. I had told my husband and my father, as well as my best friends, who came to our rescue that terrible night. I confided in a few other close friends and family as well because I thought I might need the support. It all felt a bit like atonement.

My husband Jason was an amazing stanchion through all of this. Not only was he an enthusiastic supporter of my own sobriety, he kicked the habit himself. I often look back and wonder if I would have been as successful in this journey without that shared commitment. I didn't have to contend with temptation or isolation like many do when their loved ones or partners continue to drink after they have left it behind.

In addition to the accountability, I knew I was going to need something to replace that evening at-home cocktail I had gotten used to unwinding with. I opted for a strongly brewed cinnamon tea. Not only did it have the same burn, but it actually was more relaxing and soothing to drink. Of course, there was no associated "buzz," but just having something else to put in my hand helped immensely.

Almost immediately, I began sleeping better and feeling more rested. The National Institute of Health has conducted studies on the effect of alcohol on sleep. While alcohol does act as a sedative/depressant, alcohol use and dependence are associated with "chronic sleep disturbance, lower slow wave sleep, and more rapid eye movement sleep than normal..."[10] Further, "[s]tudies show a high comorbidity of insomnia and alcoholism."[11]

Sleep is so important to overall health and wellness, not to mention your resiliency and stress tolerance. Add to that being chronically under-rested as a parent to four young kids, and

I was again hamstringing myself. Once the alcohol cleared my system, my sleep improved, and I had better sleep hygiene overall.

While many aspects of my newfound sobriety were positive, one drawback was that I started experiencing much more acute anxiety. I felt so discouraged. I had given up the bad thing. It was supposed to get better. Instead, I was confronted with all these icky feelings all the time. *What the hell?*

What I realized was that I had been using alcohol to mask my anxiety. I hadn't been really feeling it. I used alcohol to numb it down or distract from it, and I wasn't dealing with the root cause of the problem.

Better sleep helped, but I needed a bit more. I had a lot of extra energy because I wasn't fighting hangovers on the weekend or feeling sluggish because I slept poorly. I decided to invest that energy into exercise.

I had read about this thing called a "run streak." A run streak is running a prescribed distance every day without letting a day go by without running that distance. I aimed for a one-mile-per-day run streak. I was not a complete novice runner, so a mile felt accessible. I also knew it wouldn't overload my body and make the run streak unwieldy.

I posted the runs to social media because, again, accountability. What I was not prepared for was how many cheerleaders I would have along the way. People became very invested in those run streaks, and some even tried it out for themselves.

I learned so much about myself during that streak; I learned I can do hard things, that I was even more stubborn than I thought, and that dragging my pajama-clad butt out of bed at ten fifteen at night to get a late mile in on the treadmill was evidence of that stubbornness.

I learned to really enjoy running. I learned new routes through my neighborhood. I ran miles on paved paths and dirt roads, in the woods, by lakes. I even ran a *very chilly* mile across the lake on New Year's Eve 2019 when we were up at the cabin, where snow was deep, and the north sky was dark, and the snowmobile tracks I had been following disappeared into nothingness. This was more than ominous, so I hightailed it back to the safety and warmth of the cabin and finished the rest of that mile on the plowed dirt road. I learned to love the part of myself who could do those things.

It turned out that being active was also great at helping manage my anxiety. I felt better when I ran. I rose earlier; my day was more productive. It almost felt as if my brain functioned better—and, likely, it did.

The prospect of social events or professional events is daunting when you are in recovery. And in the lawyering profession, many of those events come with alcohol baked in. At first, I used the crutch of soda water with lime. If you have a drink in your hand already, no one really notices that you "aren't drinking." However, that didn't really feel right to me. I wasn't out here to fool anyone. I didn't want to feel ashamed. Sometimes, the best way to cure those feelings is to drag them into the light. So, I started talking about it more.

One of my extracurriculars for my first eight years of practice was a District Justice for District X for Phi Alpha Delta Law Fraternity, International. Part of my responsibilities in that role was to put together a leadership conference twice a year for law students and alumni members from North Dakota, Minnesota, and Wisconsin. I hadn't intended to discuss my few-months-old sobriety at this spring leadership conference, but as I looked out on the faces of my friends and colleagues in the alumni and the fresher faces of the law students, it just came out of me. I discussed my choices and my reasoning and offered to be a support to anyone going through similar struggles.

The response was overwhelmingly positive, except for one. The current International Justice of the fraternity was chatting with me in the hallway on a break. He was razzing me about the run streak and morning routine my husband and I did together and then brought up the fact that I had quit drinking as well. He joked about how I was showing everyone up with all my healthful choices. I pointed out to him that while he was a good friend and I knew he was joking, it would have been a terrible thing for a student to overhear him say to me. And if I really had been struggling in my recovery, who knows the impact that could have had?

What I will never forget from that day, and an experience that really helped solidify my choice to share and keep sharing, was a student who approached me after the conference. He said he had been thinking more about his own relationship with alcohol, and that hearing my story helped solidify his decision to reduce his alcohol consumption. This alone made sharing worth it.

The first major hurdle was over. I had shared my sobriety in a professional setting, and it went well. I hadn't been shunned, and the world didn't end. Maybe some people were silently judging me, but I had reached someone and that person benefitted from hearing my story.

According to *The Path to Lawyer Well-Being*, "[r]esearch shows that the most effective way to reduce stigma is through direct contact with someone who has personally experienced a relevant disorder. Ideally, this person should be a practicing lawyer or law student (depending on the audience) in order to create a personal connection that lends credibility and combats stigma."[12]

So, I kept sharing. I shared with people one-on-one, and I shared in groups. I joined the Well-Being Committee at the Minnesota State Bar Association to help advance lawyer well-being statewide.

In the five years since I quit drinking, I have started my own firm, developing a mission, vision, and core values as well as systems and operating procedures. I also started adjunct teaching a course on law firm ownership at the local law school. I have discovered a love of the business of law that rivals my love of practicing law.

I have also taken my love of running and passed it on to my kids. I signed up to coach track for the elementary community athletic program. That led to coaching softball and cross country and track every season ever since. Coaching youth sports fills my cup in a way I never anticipated, and I love getting to spend that time with my kids.

Eliminating alcohol has been the single most important thing I have done for my family, my career, and my health. While I can honestly say I really don't miss drinking, and I especially don't miss the hangovers, what I was not prepared for was the impact giving up drinking would have on how I understood myself.

This past summer, I was participating in a sober support group at the annual convention for the Minnesota Association for Justice—the very same organization that my father has been a member of for years and an event where a lot of hard-working trial attorneys come to play hard. What I realized in that room with my fellow sober enthusiasts was that each year that passes since I stopped drinking, I become more and more of my authentic self. And I worry less and less about what anyone else thinks.

Not everyone needs to be a complete teetotaler to benefit from reducing alcohol consumption. But don't forget that you don't have to be an alcoholic to quit drinking. My sobriety has made me stronger, more deeply rooted in myself, more present for my kids, and more loving toward my husband. It also feels good knowing I'm more capable and competent for my clients. As much as that last night of drinking pains me to reflect on, I am forever grateful I went through that and how I came out the other side.

---

1. American Bar Association, *The Path to Lawyer Well-Being: Practical Recommendations for Positive Change.* (ABA Commission on Lawyer Assistance Programs; ABA Working Group to Advance Well-Being in the Legal Profession, 2017), 7.

2. Id.

3. Id.

4. Id.

5. Id.

6. Grant BF, Chou SP, Saha TD, et al. "Prevalence of 12-Month Alcohol Use, High-Risk Drinking, and *DSM-IV* Alcohol Use Disorder in the United States, 2001-2002 to 2012-2013: Results From the National Epidemiologic Survey on Alcohol and Related Conditions." *JAMA Psychiatry.* 2017; 74(9):911–923. doi:10.1001/jamapsychiatry.2017.2161

7. MN Rules & ABA Model rules

8. ABA model rules

9. American Bar Association, *The Path to Lawyer Well-Being: Practical Rec-ommendations for Positive Change.* (ABA Commission on Lawyer Assistance Programs; ABA Working Group to Advance Well-Being in the Legal Profession, 2017), 13.

10. Colrain IM, Nicholas CL, Baker FC. "Alcohol and the sleeping brain." *Handb Clin Neurol.* 2014; 125:415-31.

11. Id.

12. American Bar Association, *The Path to Lawyer Well-Being: Practical Rec-ommendations for Positive Change.* (ABA Commission on Lawyer Assistance Programs; ABA Working Group to Advance Well-Being in the Legal Profession, 2017), 13.

Sarah Soucie Eyberg

S arah Soucie Eyberg is the principal attorney of Soucie Eyberg Law, LLC, practicing exclusively in the area of Social Security Disability law. Her dedication to professional excellence, development, and service knows practically no bounds (just ask her husband). She is a member of several local and statewide legal organizations, and serves in leadership roles in nearly every organization.

Sarah is a runner, knitter, deer hunter, mother, wife, and attorney living just outside the Twin Cities with her husband (Jason), four children (Esme, Mina, Roland, and Walter), cat, and chickens. When she is not working, she can be found at home with her family, trying new recipes or passing on her love of reading to her kids. She also passes all of her nerdy fandoms on to her kids, including *Doctor Who*, the Marvel universe, all things Halloween, and more.

https://www.facebook.com/mndisabilitylaw/

https://www.linkedin.com/in/sarah-soucie-eyberg-1014a642/

https://www.instagram.com/mndisabilitylawyer/

CHILDREN'S EMERGENCY SHELTER

All proceeds from this multi-author book are donated to Central Texas Table of Grace.

Central Texas Table of Grace is a 501(c)(3) non-profit organization that exists to provide emergency shelter services to the foster children and administers Grace365 Supervised Independent Living program for young adults aging out of foster care. Their support contributes to an improved quality of life for youth and their families. The organization's projects, implemented by an experienced staff, emphasize creating a caring climate for youth.

Supporting the development of self-confidence, healthful living, and good judgment, Central Texas Table of Grace provides our children with a thorough foundation for success.

Follow Central Texas Table of Grace on social media to find out more.

https://www.facebook.com/centraltexastableofgrace

https://www.instagram.com/ctxtableofgrace/

https://www.linkedin.com/company/central-texas-table-of-grace/

https://twitter.com/CTXTableOfGrace

https://www.tiktok.com/@ctxtableofgrace

Sulit Press is a boutique publishing house that provides high-touch support to thought leaders, industry shakers, and changemakers writing impactful nonfiction books. Whether you're interested in publishing your **personal memoir** or industry-specific **solo books,** or joining high-vibe, collaborative **multi-author books**, we'll help you transition from *aspiring* author to *published* author!

Founder and CEO Michelle Savage is an international best-selling author, speaker, book coach, and publisher. As the founder of Sulit Press, Michelle helps busy execs, entrepreneurs, coaches, writers, storytellers, and other go-getters make the leap from aspiring authors to published authors in half the time it takes to go it alone. She believes everyone has a story worth telling and teaches the craft of telling it well by providing personalized, hands-on, heart-centered support to every author.

Learn more at https://www.sulitpress.com/

www.ingramcontent.com/pod-product-compliance
Lightning Source LLC
Chambersburg PA
CBHW020251130626
46549CB00005B/2169